*antique collector's marks

antique collector's marks
essentials

edited by harriet wilson

foulsham
LONDON • NEW YORK • TORONTO • SYDNEY

foulsham

The Publishing House, Bennetts Close, Cippenham, Slough,
Berkshire, SL1 5AP, England

ISBN 0-572-02773-7

Cover photograph © DK Images

Originally published as *The Antique Market Browsers' Marks Guide*

Printed in Great Britain by Cox & Wyman Ltd, Reading

Contents

Introduction

With the increased interest in antiques fairs and car boot fairs, more and more people are becoming collectors of interesting pieces of silverware, porcelain or pottery. And once they are hooked on collecting, it follows that they want to know more about the items they admire and have bought for their home.

This handy guide is designed to help you to identify pieces of silver and silver plate, pottery and porcelain so that you can find out more about them, or have a better idea of their value. It is conveniently arranged so that the actual mark on the piece is your first point of reference; you can then find out its date and details of the maker. Simple to use and full of useful information, it will be invaluable in your trips to antique shops and markets.

If you want to move on to more detailed information, you can find it in other books by Foulsham:

English Silver Hallmarks (0-572-01181-4)

English Pottery and Porcelain Marks (0-572-00711-6)

The Identification and Dating of Sheffield Electroplated Wares 1843–1943 (0-572-02310-3)

SILVER

Both silver and gold have been much sought after for their beauty and usefulness since ancient times, and both, particularly gold, are quite rare. The value resulting from these properties has always proved a temptation to forgers and so marks were developed to prove which items were the real thing. In order to understand fully the significance of these marks it is important to know a little of the background. This will make your browsing far more interesting, and it will ensure that you don't overlook a really valuable piece! Keep the tables with you and you will be able to identify exactly what you have before you.

Silver Hallmarks

Hallmarks are the authenticating marks struck on all modern and most old English, Scottish and Irish silver and gold. Strictly speaking, they are the official marks confirming that the standard, or quality, of the metal is correct. More loosely, the term is also used to describe the marks which show where an item was made or tested for purity, who made it and its date.

Hallmarking dates from AD 1300 when it was declared that no piece of silver was 'to depart out of the hands of the workers' until it had been assayed (or tested) and marked with the leopard's head. The standard was to be 92.5 per cent pure silver, the same as for coinage.

The leopard's head, which was crowned until 1821, was originally a standard mark. However, when the lion passant gardant was introduced as a hallmark in 1544, it became more accurately the authoritative mark of the Goldsmiths' Company. As such, it was used by several provincial assay offices in addition to their own town mark. These were York and Newcastle, until those offices closed in 1857 and 1883 respectively; Chester until 1838 and Exeter until 1777. It has also been found on some Bristol silver from about 1720 to 1760.

The lion passant gardant first appeared in 1544 when Henry VIII debased the coinage to only one-third silver and so the new mark was struck, perhaps by the Goldsmiths' Company, to indicate that their hallmarked wares were sterling. In 1720, when the sterling standard was reintroduced (see below, Britannia standard) use of the mark was extended to all the existing provincial English assay offices, and it was adopted in both Sheffield and Birmingham when they opened in 1773. In Chester, York and Sheffield, the lion remained *gardant,* that is, looking over its shoulder, but in London it changed to being merely *passant* (looking ahead) in 1821, in Exeter in 1837, in Newcastle in 1846 and in Birmingham in 1875.

The Britannia standard was introduced in 1696 to put an end to the melting and clipping of coinage by silversmiths who had been using coins as cheap 'raw material'. The new standard for silverware was 95.8 per cent pure silver, higher than the 92.5 per cent required for coinage. New hallmarks were ordered: 'the figure of a woman commonly called Britannia' replaced the lion passant and leopard's head crowned as the standard mark, and the lion's head erased (torn off at the neck) replaced the leopard's head crowned as the mark of origin.

Since the Britannia standard silver was more expensive, some silversmiths began to clamour for the restoration of sterling. Others preferred the new higher standard because the silver was softer and therefore easier to work with, and it sold well abroad. In 1720, the old sterling standard was restored but permission was given to retain the higher Britannia standard alongside it.

Since the 1973 Hallmarking Act came into force in January 1975, the English assay offices – London, Birmingham and

Sheffield – have used the lion passant on sterling silver, while Edinburgh has used the lion rampant. All four assay offices use the Britannia mark on silver of the higher-quality Britannia standard.

Standard mark

The Maker's Mark

In order to ensure that standards were enforced, it clearly was necessary for the authorities to be able to identify any makers of substandard wares, so in 1363 it was decreed that each master goldsmith should have his own mark and each mark had to be registered. The earliest marks were mainly symbols, but later makers often incorporated initials as well, or used initials on their own. In 1696, when a new higher British standard was introduced, all makers had to re-register their marks and all had to include the first two letters of their surname. This rule lasted until 1720 when the old sterling standard was restored and, along with it, the old-style makers' marks. For a few years there was some overlap, with some makers using marks of the different types at the same time, so in 1739 all were ordered to re-register with new marks. From that date onwards, most marks consisted of the initials of the forename and surname, with only the occasional additional symbol such as a crown or a mullet.

Maker's mark

The Date Letter

Towards the end of the fifteenth century, continued complaints
about substandard wares led to a ruling that the assay master
should be responsible for maintaining the standard. This rule
probably itself resulted in the date letter system, which was
designed to make it possible to trace an offending assay master –
just as the makers' mark made it possible to trace dishonest
makers. The first full cycle of date letters in London started with
A in 1478. The letters J and V to Z were omitted and the resulting
20-year cycles continued without a break until 1696, each being
distinguished by a different style of lettering. Following London's
lead, other assay offices adopted their own date lettering marks,
including Edinburgh in 1681 and Dublin in 1638.

Until 1974, establishing the exact date of an item was
complicated by the fact that the lengths of each cycle and the year of
commencement varied from one assay office to another.
Furthermore, each assay office changed its date letter at a different
time of year. In 1975, all the remaining operational assay offices
(London, Birmingham, Sheffield and Edinburgh) adopted the same
lettering cycle and agreed to change the date letter on 1 January.
In 1986, the Dublin Assay Office followed suit and started a new
cycle, at A, on 1 January.

The Duty Mark

In 1720, a duty of 6d an ounce was levied on wrought plate. Some
silversmiths dodged paying this duty, which was levied at the time
of assay, by incorporating pieces of plate bearing hallmarks into

new items. The duty was removed in 1758 but reimposed in 1784, when a new, additional hallmark was introduced – the sovereign's head mark – specifically to prove that duty had been paid. From December 1784 until May 1786, the king's head was incuse (stamped), but from then until the duty was abolished in 1890 the head appeared in cameo (relief). The profiles of George III, George IV and William IV face to the right and that of Queen Victoria to the left. Besides the English assay offices, the duty mark was struck in Edinburgh, Glasgow and Dublin. Not every assay office bothered to change the head on the death of the monarch, and the profile of William IV sometimes appears on Victorian silver made as late as 1841.

Duty mark

Assay Offices outside London

Research into historical documents has revealed that there were once dozens of provincial centres producing marked silver items, from Barnstaple in the south-west to Leeds in the north. However, only a few survived as assay towns into the eighteenth or nineteenth centuries, namely Chester, Norwich, Newcastle, Exeter, York and Bristol. York and Norwich declined as manufacturing centres for the trade during the seventeenth century and were almost dormant by 1700, but Exeter, Newcastle and Chester continued to be active throughout the eighteenth century, using as their town marks a triple castle, three keeps and the arms of the City of Chester respectively.

By the middle of the eighteenth century, both Birmingham and Sheffield were fast becoming large manufacturing centres for the silver trade. In 1773, despite opposition from the London Goldsmith's Company, an Act of Parliament set up the Birmingham and Sheffield Assay Offices. Birmingham took an anchor as its mark and Sheffield a crown. When the Hallmarking Act came into force in 1975, the Sheffield Assay Office adopted a York rose as its mark in place of the crown.

Scotland

Scotland was not subject to the Britannia standard, but in 1720, when sterling was restored in England, the standard of silver in Scotland was raised to conform with it, and the same 6d an ounce duty was imposed.

From as far back as the fifteenth century, Edinburgh silver was stamped with a maker's mark, a town mark – then as now the triple towered castle – and a deacon's (or warden's) mark. In 1681, a date letter system was introduced, and at the same time an assay master's mark was substituted for that of the deacon. In 1759, the assay master's mark was replaced by the thistle standard mark.

Glasgow had an Incorporation of Hammermen as early as 1536, and a date letter system was adopted in 1681, though it fell into disuse in the eighteenth century. An official assay office was set up in 1819 and the lion rampant was chosen as the standard mark. The sovereign's head duty mark was also struck, and in 1914 the thistle standard mark was added. The Glasgow Assay Office closed in 1964.

Until the rise of Glasgow, Aberdeen was probably the most important trading centre in Scotland outside Edinburgh. From about 1600 onwards, various marks were used by the silversmiths, usually in the form of the letters AB, ABD or a contracted symbol, with a single or triple castle mark.

Silver was made in Banff from about 1680 to 1830. Various versions of the name, from B to BANF, were struck.

Silver made in Dundee from about 1625 to 1810 was stamped with a pot of lilies, a device based on the town arms.

Various marks were used in Perth, including the lion and banner of St John and, from the eighteenth century until about 1850, a double-headed eagle (the modern town symbol).

Silversmiths worked in Inverness from about 1640 to 1880, and besides the more usual INS abbreviation, a dromedary mark was sometimes used.

Montrose stamped a rose mark on silver from about 1650 to 1820, and Greenock a 'green oak' from about 1760 to 1840. At Wick and Tain, the brief names were usually struck in full, while Elgin was contracted to ELN or ELG and used with a mother and child device.

Ireland

The Irish silversmiths undoubtedly have the longest unbroken history of any in the British Isles, dating back to the Bronze Age craftsmen. The Dublin goldsmiths were granted a charter in 1555, which was followed by a Royal Charter in 1637. This prescribed the sterling standard, with the harp crowned as the standard mark. In 1638, a date letter system began but it was only haphazardly used. In 1730, a duty of 6d an ounce was imposed and the duty paid indicated by a figure of Hibernia. From 1806, Irish silver was struck with the king's head duty mark as well, so that the Hibernia tended to become the Dublin Assay Office mark.

Although the Dublin Assay Office has always been the only one in Ireland, there were guilds in several provincial cities. Silversmiths in Cork stamped their wares with a castle, sometimes accompanied by a ship, until the early eighteenth century, after which most seem to have used their own name punch and the word 'Sterling' or 'Starling'. A castle mark was also used in Limerick from about 1660 to 1710 when again some form of the word 'Sterling' took over.

The Use and Abuse of Hallmarks

Invaluable though hallmarks are to the silver collector as a guide to quality, date, provenance and maker, they can be misleading if they are totally relied on without any reference to the piece on which they appear. They can even lay the unwary collector open to the wiles of forgers.

Always take care when looking at the shapes of shields or outlines of the punch, the style of the town mark, standard mark or date letter, and the actual appearance and crispness of the marks as well as their position on the piece. Hallmarks are struck with very carefully made dies, which leave a sharp impression even after long years of use. A 'soft' mark is one of the signs of a faker who has not the time nor money to make high-grade dies. Of course, marks can become 'rubbed' over time, but one should certainly be suspicious of a fairly good Britannia mark alongside a very rubbed maker's mark and date letter. On the other hand, very few makers' marks are quite as crisply struck as the official hallmarks.

The placing of marks is also important. For example, a London-made tankard and cover from the seventeenth century would be marked to the right of the handle, near the rim, and across the cover, whereas a mid-eighteenth century one would be marked on the base. Until 1780, spoons and forks were marked near the bowl end; after that they were marked near the end of the stem.

Remember that not all good antique silver bears full hallmarks. Assay offices sometimes made mistakes, omitting, say, the date letter and striking the lion passant twice. In addition, pieces made to special order were not always sent for assay, because the law only applied to pieces 'set for sale'.

Besides being misled as to date, maker or provenance, it is possible to mistake whether a particular item is silver at all. The status of the hallmark led to many imitations, first among pewterers and later by the makers of plated goods. Many marks on Old Sheffield plate and close-plated wares and, from around 1860, on electroplated wares, look quite like silver marks. The degree of imitation on Sheffield plate led to restrictions such that from 1784 most Sheffield plate marks include the maker's full name. Electroplated wares sometimes carry marks which resemble silver hallmarks, but you will usually also find the letters EP, EPNS (on nickel plate) or EPBM (on Britannia metal). On items that have seen much use, it is also often possible to detect the base metal core.

The Hallmarking Act

The reason for hallmarking is to protect purchasers against fraud. There have been various pieces of legislation over hundreds of years designed to achieve this result. Today hallmarking is governed by the Hallmarking Act of 1973, which has simplified them and made them easier to understand. The Act came into force on 1 January 1975 and governs the hallmarking of silver, gold and platinum at the four UK assay offices – London, Birmingham, Sheffield and Edinburgh.

The main points to note are:

- Hallmarks must now consist of a maker's (or sponsor's) mark, the standard mark, the assay mark and the date letter. (Edinburgh uses the lion rampant for sterling silver.)
- All silver items weighing more than 7.8g must be hallmarked (1g for gold, 0.5g for platinum).

The Marks on Gold

Until 1798, the marks used on gold were the same as those for silver. From that date on, both 18 ct and 22 ct gold were permitted and were to be indicated by the relevant figures (.916 for 22 ct and .750 for 18 ct gold) and by a crown, which replaced the lion passant standard mark.

In 1854, three lower standards were introduced, which were indicated by the carat number plus the value in decimals: 9 with .375, 12 with .5, 15 with .625. The crown mark was reserved for 18 ct and 22 ct standards.

In 1931, 12 ct and 15 ct were replaced by 14 ct (.585).

In Sheffield, which has been licensed to assay goldwares since 1903, the gold mark is a rose. Edinburgh uses the thistle on 18 ct and 22 ct gold instead of the crown. In Glasgow, until its closure in 1964, the lion rampant appeared on all permitted standards.

In Ireland, from 1784, there have been three standards for gold – 22 ct marked with the figures and the crowned harp and Hibernia; 20 ct marked with the figures and a plume of feathers; 18 ct marked with the figures and a unicorn's head.

Maker's
mark

Assay
mark

Standard
mark

Date
letter

Gold marks

Gold standard marks

British   Imported

916 — *22 carat*

916 — *22 carat*

750 — *18 carat*

750 — *18 carat*

585 — *14 carat*

585 — *14 carat*

375 — *9 carat*

375 — *9 carat*

Assay offices

British   Imported

London

Birmingham

Sheffield

Edinburgh

Gold marks

Irish standard marks   Irish imported

22 carat

22 carat

20 carat

18 carat

14 carat

9 carat

18 carat

14 carat

9 carat

The Marks on Platinum

Since the introduction of legislation following the 1973 Hallmarking Act, all articles containing platinum at 950 parts per 1000 or more must bc hallmarked. Alloys below this standard may not be described as platinum.

The first year for marking platinum was 1975, starting with the letter A.

Maker's mark

Platinum mark

Assay mark

Date letter

Platinum marks

Standard marks		Assay office	
British	Imported	British	Imported

London

Birmingham

Sheffield

21

Introduction to the Tables

The tables on the following pages will enable you to discover much more about the pieces of silver that you come across.

The first set of tables (see pages 23–108) show the assay office marks of London, Birmingham, Chester, Dublin, Edinburgh, Exeter, Glasgow, Newcastle, Norwich, Sheffield and York. You will notice that each date letter cycle is contained in a separate box. At the outside edge of each box is a panel containing enlarged illustrations of the relevant assay office symbol and a sample date letter in the style of the boxed cycle. This should help you to find where to look for the actual mark you want, just by flipping through the pages. The side panel of each box also contains details of the monarchs reigning at the time.

The second set of tables (see pages 109–72) contains a large selection of makers' marks from 1697 to 1900. Most of them belong to London silversmiths, but the most important makers from Birmingham, Dublin, Edinburgh and Sheffield have also been included.

Our reference source has been the official records held by the Goldsmith's Company in London, whose permission and kind assistance we had in being allowed to photograph the marks. It should be noted that while every individual entry is accurate, they are not proportionally accurate to one another since all have been enlarged to a size appropriate to these pages, whatever their original size.

London

1544	G	👑	🦁		👑
1545	H	👑	🦁		Henry VIII 1547 Edward VI 1553 Mary
1546	I				
1547	K				G
1548	L		🦁		
1549	M				
1550	N		🦁		
1551	O	👑	🦁		
1552	P		🦁		
1553	Q				
1554	R				
1555	S				
1556	T				
1557	V		🦁		

Eliz. I	1558		1564	1572	
	1559		1565	1573	
	1560		1566	1574	
	1561		1567	1575	
	1562		1568	1576	
	1563		1569	1577	
			1570		
			1571		

Eliz. I	1578		1585	1592	
	1579		1586	1593	
	1580		1587	1594	
	1581		1588	1595	
	1582		1589	1596	
	1583		1590	1597	
	1584		1591		

		1605	h	1613	Q	
1598	A	1606	I	1614	R	Eliz. I
1599	B	1607	K	1615	S	1603
1600	C	1608	L	1616	T	James I
1601	D	1609	M	1617	V	
1602	E	1610	N			
1603	F	1611	O			
1604	G	1612	P			A

		1625	h	1633	q	
1618	a	1626	i	1634	r	James I
1619	b	1627	k	1635	s	1625
1620	c	1628	l	1636	t	Charles I
1621	d	1629	m	1637	v	
1622	e	1630	n			
1623	f	1631	o			
1624	g	1632	p			a

Charles I	1638		1645		1652	
1649 Charles II	1639		1646		1653	
	1640		1647		1654	
	1641		1648		1655	
	1642		1649		1656	
	1643		1650		1657	
	1644		1651			

Charles II	1658		1665		1672	
	1659		1666		1673	
	1660		1667		1674	
	1661		1668		1675	
	1662		1669		1676	
	1663		1670		1677	
	1664		1671			

		1683		1691	Charles II
1678		1684		1692	
1679		1685		1693	1685 James II
		1686		1694	1689 Wm. & My.
1680		1687		1695	1694 William III
1681		1688		1696	
1682		1689		1697	
		1690			

		1702	1710	William III
1697		1703	1711	
1698		1704	1712	1702 Anne
		1705	1713	
		1706	1714	1714 George I
1699		1707	1715	
1700		1708		
1701		1709		

27

George I	1716	Ⓐ	1721	🅕	Though not compulsory after 1720, the Britannia standard was sometimes used as an alternative standard. The identifying marks are to be found between 1720 and the present time. A piece of Britannia silver assayed in 1721 would therefore carry the marks
	1717	Ⓑ	1722	🅖	
	1718	Ⓒ	1723	🅗	
	1719	Ⓓ			
	1720	Ⓔ	1724	Ⓘ	
			1725	Ⓚ	

	1726	Ⓛ	1732	Ⓡ	Between 1719 and 1729 one should expect to find numerous variations of the leopard's head and lion passant marks.
	1727	Ⓜ	1733	Ⓢ	
	1728	Ⓝ	1734	Ⓣ	
	1729	Ⓞ	1735	Ⓥ	
	1730	Ⓟ	Between 1716 and 1728, one should expect to find an occasional variation of the shield shape:		
	1731	Ⓠ			

28

1736	1742	1750	George II
1737	1743	1751	
1738	1744	1752	
1739	1745	1753	
1740	1746	1754	
1741	1747	1755	
	1748		
	1749		

1756	1763	1771	George II
1757	1764	1772	1760 George III
1758	1765	1773	
1759	1766	1774	
1760	1767	1775	
1761	1768		
1762	1769		
	1770		

LONDON 1776–1815

George III	1776	a	1783	h	1791	q
	1777	b	1784	i	1792	r
	1778	c	1785	k	1793	s
	1779	d	1786	l	1794	t
	1780	e	1787	m	1795	u
	1781	f	1788	n		
a	1782	g	1789	o		
			1790	p		

An alternative shield may be found:

George III	1796	A	1803	H	1811	Q
	1797	B	1804	I	1812	R
	1798	C	1805	K	1813	S
	1799	D	1806	L	1814	T
	1800	E	1807	M	1815	U
	1801	F	1808	N		
A	1802	G	1809	O		
			1810	P		

An alternative shield may be found:

30

	1821	f	1828	n	
1816 a	1822 g	1829 o	George III	
1817 b	1823 h	1830 p	1820 George IV	
1818 c	1824 i	1831 q	1830 William IV	
1819 d	1825 k	1832 r		
1820 e	1826 l	1833 s		
	1827 m	1834 t		
		1835 u	a	

	1843 H	1851 Q		
1836 A	1844 J	1852 R	William IV	
1837 B	1845 K	1853 S	1837 Victoria	
1838 C	1846 L	1854 T		
1839 D	1847 M	1855 U		
1840 E	1848 N			
1841 F	1849 O	An alternative shield may be found:		
1842 G	1850 P		A	

Victoria	1856	1863		1871	
	1857	1864		1872	
	1858	1865		1873	
	1859	1866		1874	
	1860	1867		1875	
	1861	1868			
	1862	1869		An alternative shield may be found:	
		1870			

Victoria	1876	1883		1891	
	1877	1884		1892	
	1878	1885		1893	
	1879	1886		1894	
	1880	1887		1895	
	1881	1888			
	1882	1889			
		1890			

		1903	h	1911	q
1896	a	1904	i	1912	r
1897	b	1905	k	1913	s
1898	c	1906	l	1914	t
1899	d	1907	m	1915	u
1900	e	1908	n		Victoria
1901	f	1909	o		1901 Edward VII
1902	g	1910	p		1910 George V

a

		1923	h	1931	q
1916	a	1924	i	1932	r
1917	b	1925	k	1933	s
1918	c	1926	l	1934	t
1919	d	1927	m	1935	u
1920	e	1928	n		George V
1921	f	1929	o		
1922	g	1930	p		

The Britannia standard marks for 1927:

a

(leopard head mark)	(lion mark)	(head mark)	1943	H	1951	Q
	1936	A	1944	I	(lion, leopard, head marks)	
1936 Ewd. VIII	1937	B	1945	K	1952	R
1936 George VI	1938	C	1946	L	1953	S
1952 Eliz. II	1939	D	1947	M	(lion, head marks)	
	1940	E	1948	N	1954	T
	1941	F	1949	O	1955	U
A	1942	G	1950	P		

(head mark)	(lion mark)	(head mark)	1963	h	1971	q
Eliz. II	1956	a	1964	i	1972	r
	1957	b	1965	k	This sequence was discontinued after the 1973 Hallmarking Act.	
	1958	c	1966	l		
	1959	d	1967	m	1973	s
	1960	e	1968	n	1974	t
	1961	f	1969	o		
a	1962	g	1970	p		

		1983	𝒢	1992	𝒮	Eliz. II
1975	𝒜	1984	𝒦	1993	𝒯	
1976	ℬ	1985	ℒ	1994	𝒰	
1977	𝒞	1986	ℳ	1995	𝒱	
1978	𝒟	1987	𝒩	1996	𝒲	
1979	ℰ	1988	𝒪	1997	𝒳	
1980	ℱ	1989	𝒫	1998	𝒴	
1981	𝒢	1990	𝒬	1999	𝒵 2000	𝒜
1982	ℋ	1991	ℛ			
2000	a 2000					
2001	b					
2002	c					a

35

Birmingham

George III	🦁	⚓	1781	I	1790	S
	1773	A	1782	K	1791	T
	1774	B	1783	L	1792	U
	1775	C	1784	M	1793	V
	1776	D	1785	N	1794	W
	1777	E	1786	O	1795	X
	1778	F	1787	P	1796	Y
	1779	G	1788	Q	1797	Z
A	1780	H	1789	R	July 1797–March 1780: the King's head is duplicated.	

George III **1820** **George IV**	🦁	⚓	👤	1806	i	1815	r
	1798	a		1807	j	1816	s
	1799	b		1808	k	1817	t
	1800	c		1809	l	1818	u
	1801	d		1810	m	1819	v
	1802	e		1811	n	1820	w
	1803	f		1812	o	1821	x
a	1804	g		1813	p	1822	y
	1805	h		1814	q	1823	z

Lion	Anchor	Head	Year	Letter	Year	Letter	Monarch / Anchor
🦁	⚓	👤	1832	J	1841	S	⚓
1824	A		1833	K	1842	T	
1825	B		1834	L 👤	1843	U	George IV
1826	C		1835	M	1844	V	1830 William IV
1827	D		1836	N	1845	W	1837 Victoria
1828	E		1837	O	1846	X	
1829	F		1838	P 👤	1847	Y	
1830	G		1839	Q	1848	Z	
1831	H 👤		1840	R			A

Lion	Anchor	Head	Year	Letter	Lion	Anchor	Head	Year	Letter	Monarch / Anchor
🦁	⚓	👤	1858	J	🦁	⚓	👤	1867	S	⚓
1849	A				1859	K		1868	T	Victoria
1850	B				1860	L		1869	U	
1851	C				1861	M		1870	V	
1852	D				1862	N		1871	W	
1853	E				1863	O		1872	X	
1854	F				1864	P		1873	Y	
1855	G				1865	Q		1874	Z	
1856	H				1866	R				⚓
1857	I									

⚓ Victoria	🦁	👑	👤	🦁	👑	👤	1891	ⓡ
	1875	ⓐ		1883	ⓘ		1892	ⓢ
	1876	ⓑ		1884	ⓚ		1893	ⓣ
	1877	ⓒ		1885	ⓛ		1894	ⓤ
	1878	ⓓ		1886	ⓜ		1895	ⓥ
	1879	ⓔ		1887	ⓝ		1896	ⓦ
	1880	ⓕ		1888	ⓞ		1897	ⓧ
	1881	ⓖ		1889	ⓟ		1898	ⓨ
ⓐ	1882	ⓗ		1890	ⓠ		1899	ⓩ

⚓ Victoria	👑	🦁		1908	ⓘ		1917	ⓢ
1901 Ewd. VII	1900	ⓐ		1909	ⓚ	⚓		🦁
	1901	ⓑ		1910	ⓛ		1918	ⓣ
1910 George V	1902	ⓒ		1911	ⓜ		1919	ⓤ
	1903	ⓓ		1912	ⓝ		1920	ⓥ
	1904	ⓔ		1913	ⓞ		1921	ⓦ
ⓐ	1905	ⓕ		1914	ⓟ		1922	ⓧ
	1906	ⓖ		1915	ⓠ		1923	ⓨ
	1907	ⓗ		1916	ⓡ		1924	ⓩ

				1940	Q	George V
1925	A	1933	J	1941	R	1935 Ewd. VIII
1926	B	1934	K	1942	S	
1927	C	1935	L	1943	T	
1928	D	1936	M	1944	U	
1929	E	1937	N	1945	V	
1930	F	1938	O	1946	W	
1931	G	1939	P	1947	X	
1932	H			1948	Y	
				1949	Z	A
1950	A	1954	E	1960	L	George VI
1951	B	1955	F	1961	M	1952 Eliz. II
1952	C	1956	G	1962	N	
1953	D	1957	H	1963	O	
		1958	J	1964	P	
		1959	K	1965	2	A

39

Eliz. II	1966	1967	1968		1969	1970	1971		1972	1973	1974
	R	*S*	*T*		*T*	*U*	*V*		*X*	*Y*	*Z*

R

Eliz. II	1975	1976	1977	1978	1979	1980	1981	1982		1983	1984	1985	1986	1987	1988	1989	1990		1991	1992	1993	1994	1995	1996	1997	1998	1999
	A	*B*	*C*	*D*	*E*	*F*	*G*	*H*		*I*	*K*	*L*	*M*	*N*	*O*	*P*	*Q*		*R*	*S*	*T*	*U*	*V*	*W*	*X*	*Y*	*Z*

A

Eliz. II	2000	2001	2002
	a	*b*	*c*

Chester

1680		1690		1690–1700	Charles II 1685 James II 1689 Wm. & My. 1694 William III
1701 A 1702 B 1703 C 1704 D 1705 E 1706 F 1707 G 1708 H		1709 I 1710 K 1711 L 1712 M 1713 N 1714 O 1715 P 1716 Q 1717 R		1718 S 1719 T 1720 U 1721 V 1722 W 1723 X 1724 Y 1725 Z	William III 1702 Anne 1714 George I A

		1734	🅙	1743	🅙
	1726 🅐	1735	🅚	1744	🅙
	1727 🅑	1736	🅛	1745	🅤
George I	1728 🅒	1737	🅜	1746	🅥
1727 George II	1729 🅓	1738	🅝	1747	🅦
	1730 🅔	1739	🅞	1748	🅧
	1731 🅕	1740	🅟	1749	🅨
	1732 🅖	1741	🅠	1750	🅩
🅐	1733 🅗	1742	🅡		

		1759	ⓘ	1768	🆂
	1751 ⓐ	1760	ⓚ	1769	🆃
	1752 ⓑ	1761	ⓛ	1770	🆃
George II	1753 ⓒ	1762	ⓜ	1771	🆄
1760 George III	1754 ⓓ	1763	ⓝ	1772	🆅
	1755 ⓔ	1764	ⓞ	1773	🆆
	1756 ⓕ	1765	ⓟ	1774	🆇
	1757 ⓖ	1766	ⓠ	1775	🆈
ⓐ	1758 ⓗ	1767	ⓡ		

1776 ⓐ	1782 ⓖ	1789 ⓞ	
1777 ⓑ	1783 ⓗ	1790 ⓟ	
1778 ⓒ	1784 ⓘ	1791 ⓠ	
1779 ⓓ	1785 ⓚ	1792 ⓡ	George III
1780 ⓔ	1786 ⓛ	1793 ⓢ	
1781 ⓕ	1787 ⓜ	1794 ⓣ	
	1788 ⓝ	1795 ⓤ	
		1796 ⓥ	ⓐ

1797 Ⓐ	1803 Ⓖ	1811 Ⓟ	
1798 Ⓑ	1804 Ⓗ	1812 Ⓠ	
1799 Ⓒ	1805 Ⓘ	1813 Ⓡ	
1800 Ⓓ	1806 Ⓚ	1814 Ⓢ	
1801 Ⓔ	1807 Ⓛ	1815 Ⓣ	George III
1802 Ⓕ	1808 Ⓜ	1816 Ⓤ	
	1809 Ⓝ	1817 Ⓥ	
	1810 Ⓞ		Ⓐ

George III		1824 **F**	1833 **P**
1818 **A**		1825 **G**	1834 **Q**
1819 **B**		1826 **H**	1835 **R**
George III	1820 **C**	1827 **I**	1836 **S**
1820 George IV	1821 **D**	1828 **K**	1837 **T**
1830 William IV	1822 **D**	1829 **L**	1838 **U**
1837 Victoria		1830 **M**	
Ā	1823 **E**	1831 **N**	
		1832 **O**	

Victoria	1839 **A**	1847 **J**	1856 **S**
	1840 **B**	1848 **K**	1857 **T**
	1841 **C**	1849 **L**	1858 **U**
	1842 **D**	1850 **M**	1859 **V**
	1843 **E**	1851 **N**	1860 **W**
	1844 **F**	1852 **O**	1861 **X**
	1845 **G**	1853 **P**	1862 **Y**
A	1846 **H**	1854 **Q**	1863 **Z**
		1855 **R**	

1864 **a**	1871 **h**	1879 **q**	Victoria
1865 **b**	1872 **i**	1880 **r**	
1866 **c**	1873 **k**	1881 **s**	
1867 **d**	1874 **l**	1882 **t**	
1868 **e**	1875 **m**	1883 **u**	
1869 **f**	1876 **n**		
1870 **g**	1877 **o**		**a**
	1878 **p**		

1884 **A**	1890 **G**	1897 **O**	Victoria
1885 **B**	1891 **H**	1898 **P**	
1886 **C**	1892 **I**	1899 **Q**	
1887 **D**	1893 **K**	1900 **R**	
1888 **E**	1894 **L**	An alternative sterling mark used since 1839:	
1889 **F**	1895 **M**	An alternative date letter shield used since 1900:	**A**
	1896 **N**		

45

Ewd. VII			1908	🄷	1917	🄰	
	1901	🄰	1909	🄸	1918	🄻	
1910 George V	1902	🄱	1910	🄺	1919	🄹	
	1903	🄲	1911	🄻	1920	🄴	
	1904	🄳	1912	🄼	1921	🄽	
	1905	🄴	1913	🄽	1922	🅆	
	1906	🄵	1914	🄾	1923	🅇	
	1907	🄶	1915	🄿	1924	🅈	
			1916	🅀	1925	🅉	

George V			1933	🄷	1940	🄿
	1926	🄰	1934	🄸	1941	🅀
1936 Ewd. VIII	1927	🄱	1935	🄺	1942	🅁
	1928	🄲	1936	🄻	1943	🅂
1936 George VI	1929	🄳	1936	🄻	1944	🅃
	1930	🄴	1937	🄼	1945	🅄
	1931	ff	1938	🄽	1946	🅅
	1932	🄶	1939	🄾	1947	🅆

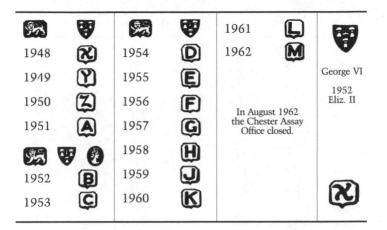

1948		1954	D	1961	L
1949	Y	1955	E	1962	M
1950	Z	1956	F		
1951	A	1957	G		George VI
1952	B	1958	H		1952 Eliz. II
1953	C	1959	J	In August 1962 the Chester Assay Office closed.	
		1960	K		

47

Dublin

			1645	**H**	1652	**P**
					1653	**Q**
Charles I	1638	**A**	1646	**I**	1654	**R**
	1639	**B**	1647	**K**		
1649 Charles II	1640	**C**	1648	**L**		
	1641	**D**	1649	**M**	1655	**S**
	1642	**E**	1650	**N**	1656	**T**
A	1643	**F**	1651	**O**	1657	**U**
	1644	**G**				
			1665	**h**	1672	**p**
			1666	**i**	1673	**q**
Charles II	1658	**a**	1667	**k**	1674	**r**
	1659	**b**	1668	**l**	1675	**s**
	1660	**c**	1669	**m**	1676	**t**
	1661	**d**	1670	**n**	1677	**u**
	1662	**e**				
a	1663	**f**	1671	**o**		
	1664	**g**				

🦌	🦌	1688–93	🅗	1704	🅡	🦌	
1678	🅐	1694–1695	🅚	1706–1707	🅢	Charles II	
1679	🅑	1696–1698	🅛	1708–1709	🅣	1685 James II	
1680	🅒	1699	🅜	1710–1711	🅤	1689 Wm. & My.	
1681	🅓	1700	🅝	1712–1713	🅦	1694 William III	
1682	🅔	1701	🅞	🦌 1714 🅧		1702 Anne	
1683–4	🅕	1702	🅟	**1715**	🅨	1714 George I	
1685–7	🅖	1703	🅠	**1716**	🅩	🅐	
🦌	🦌	1726	🅖	1736	🅞	🦌	
1717	🅐	1727	🅗	1737	🅡	George I	
1718	🅑	1728	🅘	1738	🅢	1727 George II	
1719	🅒	1729	🅚	1739	🅣		
		1730	🅛	1740	🅦🅦		
1720	🅐	🦌	🅞	🦌	🅞		
1721	🅑	1731	🅤	1741–1742	🅦🅦		
1722	🅒	1732	🅦	1743–1744	🅧		
1723	🅓	1733	🅝	1745	🅨		
1724	🅔	1734	🅞	1746	🅩		
1725	🅕	1735	🅟	🦌 An alternative crowned harp found between 1739 and 1748.		🅐	

(crowned harp mark)	(Hibernia)	(crowned harp)	1757	I	1766	S
	1747	A	1758	K		(crowned harp)
(Hibernia seated)		(crowned harp)	1759	L	1767	T
		B		(crowned harp)	1768	U
George II	1748	C	1760	M	1769	W
1760 George III	1749	D	1761	N	1770	X
	1750	EE	1762	O	1771	Y
	1751	F	1763	P	1772	Z
	1752	G	1764	Q		
A	1753	H	1765	R		
	1754					

An alternative Hibernia found between 1752 and 1754.

		1781	Ⓘ	1790	Ⓢ	
1773	Ⓐ	1782	Ⓚ	1791	Ⓣ	
1774	Ⓑ	1783	Ⓛ	1792	Ⓤ	
1775	Ⓒ	1784	Ⓜ			George III
		1785	Ⓝ	1793	Ⓦ	
1776	Ⓓ	1786	Ⓞ	1794	Ⓧ	
1777	Ⓔ			1795	Ⓨ	
1778	Ⓕ	1787	Ⓟ	1796	Ⓩ	
1779	Ⓖ	1788	Ⓠ			
1780	Ⓗ	1789	Ⓡ			Ⓐ

51

		1806	**K**	1815	**T**
1797	**A**	1807	**L**	1816	**U**
1798	**B**	1808	**M**	1817	**W**
George III 1799	**C**	1809	**N**	1818	**X**
1820 George IV 1800	**D**	1810	**O**	1819	**Y**
1801	**E**	1811	**P**	1820	**Z**
1802	**F**	1812	**Q**		
1803	**G**	1813	**R**		
1804	**H**	1814	**S**		
A 1805	**I**				

Year	Letter				Monarch
1821	Ⓐ	⚬	⚬	⚬	⚬
1822	Ⓑ			⚬	
1823	Ⓒ				⚬
1824	Ⓓ				
1825	Ⓔⓔ				1820 George IV
1826	Ⓕ				
1827	Ⓖ	⚬	⚬	⚬	1830 William IV
1828	Ⓗ	⚬	⚬	⚬	
1829	Ⓘ	⚬	⚬	⚬	1837 Victoria
1830	Ⓚ	⚬	⚬	⚬	
1831	Ⓛ	⚬	⚬	⚬	
1832	Ⓜ				
1833	Ⓝ	⚬	⚬		
1834	Ⓞ	⚬	⚬	⚬	
1835	Ⓟ				
1836	Ⓠ				
1837	Ⓡ	⚬	⚬	⚬	
1838	Ⓢ			⚬	
1839	Ⓣ	⚬	⚬		
1840	Ⓤ				
1841	Ⓥ				
1842	Ⓦ	⚬	⚬		
1843	Ⓧ				
1844	Ⓨ	⚬	⚬		
1845	Ⓩ	⚬	⚬		Ⓐ

1846	â	1855	k	1864	t
1847	b	1856	l	1865	u
1848	c	1857	m	1866	v
1849	d	1858	n	1867	w
1850	e	1859	o	1868	x
1851	f f	1860	p	1869	y
1852	g g	1861	q	1870	z
1853	h h	1862	r		
1854	j	1863	s		

Victoria

54

🛡	🛡	👑	1880	Ⓚ	1890	Ⓤ	🏴
1871		Ⓐ	1881	Ⓛ	1891	Ⓥ	🛡
1872		Ⓑ	1882	Ⓜ	1892	Ⓦ	Victoria
1873		Ⓒ	1883	Ⓝ	1893	Ⓧ	
1874		Ⓓ	1884	Ⓞ	1894	Ⓨ	
1875		Ⓔ	1885	Ⓟ	1895	Ⓩ	
1876		Ⓕ	1886	Ⓠ			
1877		Ⓖ	1887	Ⓡ			
1878		Ⓗ	1888	Ⓢ			
1879		Ⓘ	1889	Ⓣ			Ⓐ

55

			1902	𝕲	1909	𝕺	
	1896	𝕬	1903	𝕳	1910	𝕻	
	1897	𝕭	1904	𝕱	1911	𝕼	
Victoria	1898	𝕮	1905	𝕶	1912	𝕽	
1901 Ewd. VII	1899	𝕯	1906	𝕷	1913	𝕾	
1910 George V	1900	𝕰	1907	𝕸	1914	𝕿	
	1901	𝕱	1908	𝕹	1915	𝖀	
George V 1936 Ewd. VIII 1936 George VI	1916	𝕬	1925	𝕭	1935	𝕮	
	1917	𝕓	1926	𝕝	1936	𝖀	
	1918	𝕔	1927	𝕞	1937	𝖁	
	1919	𝕕	1928	𝕟	1938	𝖂	
	1920	𝕖	1929	𝕠	1939	𝖃	
	1921	𝕗	1930	𝕡	1940	𝖄	
	1922	𝕤	1931	𝕡	1941	𝖅	
	1923	𝕙	1932	𝕢			
	1924	𝕚	1933	𝕣			
			1934	𝕤			

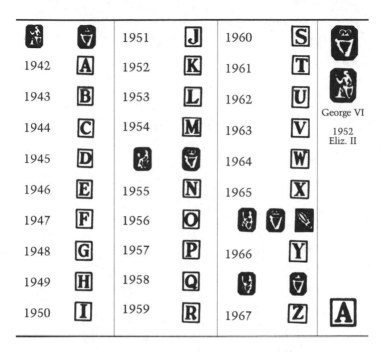

		1951	J	1960	S	
1942	A	1952	K	1961	T	
1943	B	1953	L	1962	U	
1944	C	1954	M	1963	V	George VI
1945	D			1964	W	1952 Eliz. II
1946	E	1955	N	1965	X	
1947	F	1956	O			
1948	G	1957	P	1966	Y	
1949	H	1958	Q			
1950	I	1959	R	1967	Z	A

(harp)	(figure)	(figure)	1978	m	1991	F
	1968	a	1979	n	1992	G
(figure)	1969	b	1980	o	1993	H
Eliz. II	1970	c	1981	p	1994	I
	1971	d	1982	R	1995	J
	1972	e	1983	s	1996	K
	1973	F (emblem)	1984	t	1997	L
	(figure) (emblem)		1985	u	1998	M
	1974	S	1986	A	1999	N (emblem)
	1975	h	1987	B (shield)	2000	O (emblem)
	1976	i	1988	C (shield)	2001	Q
a	1977	l	1989	D		
			1990	E		

58

Edinburgh

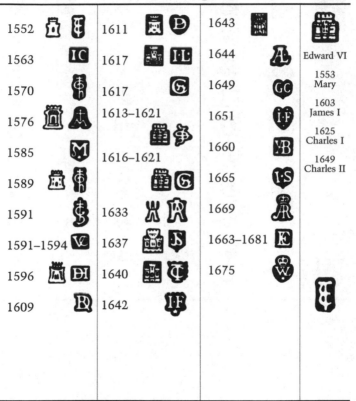

1552	1611	1643	Edward VI
1563	1617	1644	1553 Mary
1570	1617	1649	1603 James I
1576	1613–1621	1651	1625 Charles I
1585	1616–1621	1660	1649 Charles II
1589		1665	
1591	1633	1669	
1591–1594	1637	1663–1681	
1596	1640	1675	
1609	1642		

1685
James II

1689
Wm. & My.

1694
William III

1702
Anne

1681	1689			
1682	1690	1698		
1683	1691	1699		
1684	1692	1700		
1685	1693	1701		
1686	1694	1702		
1687	1695	1703		
1688	1696	1704		
	1697			

🏰	💗	1713	I	1721	R		🏰
1705	A	🏰	EP	1722	S		
1706	B	1714	K	1723	T		Anne
🏰	EP	1715	L	1724	U		1714 George I
1707	C	1716	M	1725	V		1727 George II
1708	D	1717	N	1726	W		
1709	E	🏰	EP	1727	X		
1710	F	1718	O	1728	Y		
1711	G	1719	P	1729	Z		
🏰	EP	🏰	EP				
1712	H	1720	q				A

🏰	🏰	AU	1739	𝒦	1746	𝓡
George II	1730	𝒜	🏰	GED	🏰	HG
	1731	𝓑	1740	𝓛	1747	𝓢
	1732	𝓒	1741	𝓜	1748	𝓙
	1733	𝓓	🏰	EL	1749	𝓤
	1734	𝓔	1742	𝓝	1750	𝓥
	1735	𝓕	1743	O	1751	𝓦
	1736	𝓖	🏰	HG	1752	𝓧
	1737	𝓗	1744	𝓟	1753	𝓨
𝒜	1738	𝓘	1745	2	1754	𝓩

🏰	HG	🏰	🦁	1771	R	🏰
1755	A	1763	J J	1772	S	George II
1756	B	1764	k	1773	T	1760 George III
1757	C	1765	L	1774	U	
1758	D	1766	M	1775	V	
🏰	🦁	1767	N	1776	X	
1759	E	1768	O	1777	Y	
1760	F	1769	P	1778	Z	
1761	G	1770	Q	1779	U	
1762	H	🏰 🦁	Alternative town marks sometimes found around 1771.			A

63

			1789	I J	1798	S
			1790	K		
George III					1799	T
	1780	A	1791	L		
	1781	B	1792	M	1800	U
	1782	C	1793	N N	1801	V
	1783	D	1794	O O		
	1784	E	1795	P	1802	W
	1785	F	1796	Q	1803	X
	1786	G			1804	Y
	1787	G	1797	R R	1805	Z
A	1788	H				

		Year				
🏰	🦁	1814	i	🏰	🦁	🏰
1806	a 👤	1815	J	1824	S 👤	George III
1807	b	1816	k	1825	t	1820 George IV
1808	c	1817	l	🏰	🦁	1830 William IV
🏰	🦁	1818	m	1826	u 👤	
1809	d 👤	1819	n	1827	V	
1810	e	🏰	🦁	1828	W	
1811	f	1820	o 👤	1829	X	
1812	g	1821	p	1830	Y	
🏰	🦁	1822	q	1831	Z	
1813	h 👤	1823	r			a

			1841		1851	
	1832		1842		1852	
William IV	1833		1843		1853	
1837 Victoria	1834		1844		1854	
	1835		1845		1855	
	1836		1846		1856	
	1837		1847			
	1838		1848			
	1839		1849			
	1840		1850			

🏰 🌹 🐕	1865	Ⓘ	1874	Ⓢ	🏰
1857 Ⓐ	1866	Ⓚ	🏰 🌹 🐕	Victoria
1858 Ⓑ	1867	Ⓛ	1875	Ⓣ	
1859 Ⓒ	1868	Ⓜ	1876	Ⓤ	
1860 Ⓓ	1869	Ⓝ	1877	Ⓥ	
1861 Ⓔ	1870	Ⓞ	1878	Ⓦ	
1862 Ⓕ	1871	Ⓟ	1879	Ⓧ	
1863 Ⓖ	1872	Ⓠ	1880	Ⓨ	
1864 Ⓗ	1873	Ⓡ	1881	Ⓩ	Ⓐ

Victoria	1882	ⓐ	1890	ⓘ	1898	ⓡ
1901 Ewd. VII	1883	ⓑ	1891	ⓚ	1899	ⓢ
	1884	ⓒ	1892	ⓛ	1900	ⓣ
	1885	ⓓ	1893	ⓜ	1901	ⓥ
	1886	ⓔ	1894	ⓝ	1902	ⓦ
	1887	ⓕ	1895	ⓞ	1903	ⓧ
	1888	ⓖ	1896	ⓟ	1904	ⓨ
ⓐ	1889	ⓗ	1897	ⓠ	1905	ⓩ

🏰	🌸	1914	Ⓘ	🏰	🌸	👑
1906	Ⓐ	1915	Ⓚ	1923	Ⓢ	
1907	Ⓑ	1916	Ⓛ	1924	Ⓣ	Ewd. VII
1908	Ⓒ	1917	Ⓜ	1925	Ⓤ	1910 George V
1909	Ⓓ	1918	Ⓝ	1926	Ⓥ	
1910	Ⓔ	1919	Ⓞ	1927	Ⓦ	
1911	Ⓕ	1920	Ⓟ	1928	Ⓧ	
1912	Ⓖ	1921	Ⓠ	1929	Ⓨ	
1913	Ⓗ	1922	Ⓡ	1930	Ⓩ	Ⓐ

					1948	
	1931	𝒜	1939	𝒥	1949	𝒯
Ewd. VIII	1932	ℬ	1940	𝒦	1950	𝒰
1936 George VI						
1952 Eliz. II			1941	ℒ	1951	𝒱
	1933	𝒞	1942	ℳ		
	1934	𝒟	1943	𝒩		
	1935	ℰ	1944	𝒪	1952	𝒲
	1936	ℱ	1945	𝒫	1953	𝒳
	1937	𝒢	1946	𝒬		
					1954	𝒴
	1938	ℋ	1947	ℛ	1955	𝒵

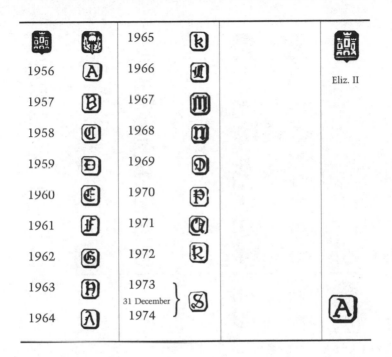

		1965	𝕜		
1956	𝔸	1966	𝕝		Eliz. II
1957	𝔹	1967	𝕞		
1958	ℂ	1968	𝕟		
1959	𝔻	1969	𝕠		
1960	𝔼	1970	𝕡		
1961	𝔽	1971	𝕢		
1962	𝔾	1972	𝕣		
1963	ℍ	1973 31 December }	𝕤		
1964	𝕁	1974			𝔸

			1983	*J*	1992	*S*
Eliz. II	1975	*A*	1984	*K*	1993	*T*
	1976	*B*	1985	*L*	1994	*U*
	1977	*C*	1986	*M*	1995	*V*
	1978	*D*	1987	*N*	1996	*W*
	1979	*E*	1988	*O*	1997	*X*
	1980	*F*	1989	*P*	1998	*Y*
	1981	*G*	1990	*Q*	1999	*Z*
A	1982	*H*	1991	*R*		
Eliz. II	2000	a				
	2001	b				
	2002	c				
a						

Exeter

 1570	 1585		 Eliz. I
 1571	 1635 1675	 1690	1603 James I 1625 Charles I
 1575	 1680	 1698	1649 Charles II 1685 James II 1694 William III
 1580			

		1709	I	1718	S
1701	A	1710	K	1719	T
Anne 1702	B	1711	L	1720	V
1714 George I 1703	C	1712	M		
1704	D	1713	N	1721	W
1705	E	1714	O	1722	X
1706	F	1715	P	1723	Y
1707	G	1716	Q	1724	Z
A 1708	H	1717	R		

1725	ⓐ	1733	Ⓘ	1741	Ⓡ	
1726	ⓑ	1734	Ⓚ	1742	Ⓢ	
1727	ⓒ	1735	Ⓛ	1743	Ⓣ	George I
1728	ⓓ	1736	Ⓜ	1744	Ⓤ	1727 George II
1729	ⓔ	1737	Ⓝ	1745	Ⓦ	
1730	ⓕ	1738	Ⓞ	1746	Ⓧ	
1731	ⓖ	1739	Ⓟ	1747	Ⓨ	
1732	ⓗ	1740	Ⓠ	1748	Ⓩ	ⓐ
1749	Ⓐ	1757	Ⓘ	1765	Ⓡ	
1750	Ⓑ	1758	Ⓚ	1766	Ⓢ	
1751	Ⓒ	1759	Ⓛ	1767	Ⓣ	George II
1752	Ⓓ	1760	Ⓜ	1768	Ⓤ	1760 George III
1753	Ⓔ	1761	Ⓝ	1769	Ⓦ	
1754	Ⓕ	1762	Ⓞ	1770	Ⓧ	
1755	Ⓖ	1763	Ⓟ	1771	Ⓨ	
1756	Ⓗ	1764	Ⓠ	1772	Ⓩ	Ⓐ

75

George III	1773 **A**	1781 **I**	1789 **q**	
	1774 **B**	1782 **I**	1790 **r**	
	1775 **C**	1783 **K**	1791 **f**	
	1776 **D**	1784 **L**	1792 **t**	
	1777 **E**	1785 **M**	1793 **u**	
	1778 **F**	1786 **N**	1794 **W**	
	1779 **G**	1787 **O**	1795 **X**	
	1780 **H**	1788 **P**	1796 **y**	

George III	1797 **A**	1804 **H**	1811 **P**
	1798 **B**	1805 **I**	1812 **Q**
	1799 **C**	1806 **K**	1813 **R**
	1800 **D**	1807 **L**	1814 **S**
	1801 **E**	1808 **M**	1815 **T**
	1802 **F**	1809 **N**	1816 **U**
	1803 **G**	1810 **O**	

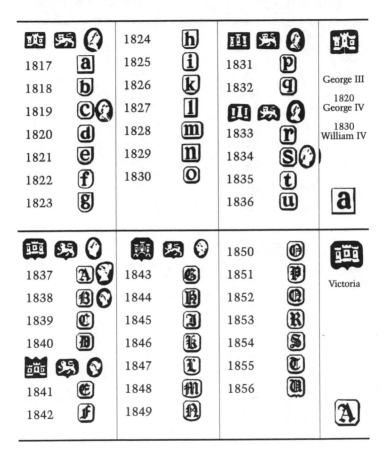

1824	h
1825	i
1826	k
1827	l
1828	m
1829	n
1830	o

1817	a
1818	b
1819	c
1820	d
1821	e
1822	f
1823	g

1831	p
1832	q
1833	r
1834	s
1835	t
1836	u

George III

1820
George IV

1830
William IV

1837	A
1838	B
1839	C
1840	D
1841	E
1842	F

1843	G
1844	H
1845	I
1846	K
1847	L
1848	M
1849	N

1850	O
1851	P
1852	Q
1853	R
1854	S
1855	T
1856	U

Victoria

77

Victoria	(book) (lion) (head)		1864	H	1872	Q
	1857	A	1865	I	1873	R
	1858	B	1866	K	1874	S
	1859	C	1867	L	1875	T
	1860	D	1868	M	1876	U
	1861	E	1869	N		
	1862	F	1870	O		
A	1863	G	1871	P		

Victoria	(book) (lion) (head)	
	1877	A
	1878	B
	1879	C
	1880	D
	1881	E
A	1882	F
	In 1883, the Exeter Assay Office closed.	

Glasgow

1681	**a**	1694	**O**	1700	**U**	
		1696	**Q**	1701	**V**	Charles II
				1704	**Y**	1685 James II
1683	**C**			1705	**Z**	1689 Wm. & My.
1685	**E**	1698	**S**			1694 William III
						1702 Anne
1689	**U**			1707	**B**	
1690	**K**	1699	**t**			
				1709	**D**	

a

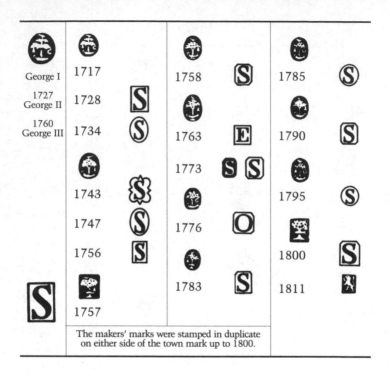

The makers' marks were stamped in duplicate on either side of the town mark up to 1800.

George I	1717		1758	1785	
1727 George II	1728				
1760 George III	1734		1763	1790	
	1743		1773	1795	
	1747		1776	1800	
	1756			1811	
	1757		1783		

80

1819	Ⓐ	1827	Ⓘ	1837	Ⓢ	George IV
1820	Ⓑ	1828	Ⓙ	1838	Ⓣ	1830 William IV
1821	Ⓒ	1829	Ⓚ	1839	Ⓤ	1837 Victoria
1822	Ⓓ	1830	Ⓛ	1840	Ⓥ	
1823	Ⓔ	1831	Ⓜ	1841	Ⓦ	
1824	Ⓕ	1832	Ⓝ	1842	Ⓧ	
1825	Ⓖ	1833	Ⓠ	1843	Ⓨ	
1826	Ⓗ	1834	Ⓟ	1844	Ⓩ	
		1835	Ⓠ			
		1836	Ⓡ			Ⓐ

Victoria							1862	R	
	1845	A		1853	I		1863	S	
	1846	B		1854	J		1864	T	
	1847	C		1855	K		1865	U	
	1848	D		1856	L		1866	V	
	1849	E		1857	M		1867	W	
	1850	F		1858	N		1868	X	
	1851	G		1859	O		1869	Y	
A	1852	H		1860	P		1870	Z	
				1861	Q				

🛡️	🦁	🌐	1879	Ⓘ	1888	Ⓡ	🛡️	
1871	Ⓐ		1880	Ⓙ	1889	Ⓢ	Victoria	
1872	Ⓑ		1881	Ⓚ	1890	Ⓣ		
1873	Ⓒ		1882	Ⓛ	1891	Ⓤ		
1874	Ⓓ		1883	Ⓜ	1892	Ⓥ		
1875	Ⓔ		1884	Ⓝ	1893	Ⓦ		
1876	Ⓕ		1885	Ⓞ	1894	Ⓧ		
1877	Ⓖ		1886	Ⓟ	1895	Ⓨ		
1878	Ⓗ		1887	Ⓠ	1896	Ⓩ	Ⓐ	

			1906	𝔡			
Victoria	1897	𝒜	1907	𝒦	1914	𝓡	
1901 Ewd. VII	1898	𝓑	1908	𝓛	1915	𝓢	
1910 George V	1899	𝓒			1916	𝓣	
	1900	𝓓	1909	𝓜	1917	𝓤	
	1901	𝓔	1910	𝓝	1918	𝓥	
	1902	𝓕	1911	𝓠	1919	𝓦	
	1903	𝓖			1920	𝓧	
	1904	𝓚	1912	𝓟	1921	𝓨	
𝒜	1905	𝓙	1913	𝟐	1922	𝓩	

🛡️🦁🌸	1932 j	1941 s	🛡️
1923 a	1933 k	1942 t	George V
1924 b	🛡️🦁🌸😊	1943 u	1936 Ewd. VIII
1925 c	1934 l	1944 v	1936 George VI
1926 d	1935 m	🛡️🦁🌸	
1927 e	🛡️🦁🌸	1945 w	
1928 f	1936 n	1946 x	
1929 g	1937 o	1947 y	
🛡️🦁🌸	1938 p	1948 z	
1930 h	1939 q		
1931 i	1940 r		a

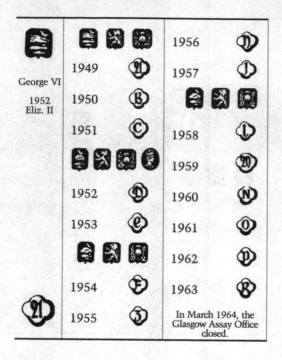

George VI	1949	1956
1952 Eliz. II	1950	1957
	1951	1958
	1952	1959
	1953	1960
	1954	1961
	1955	1962
		1963

In March 1964, the Glasgow Assay Office closed.

Newcastle

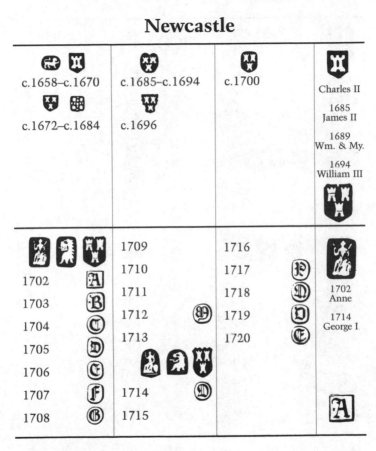

c.1658–c.1670	c.1685–c.1694	c.1700	Charles II
c.1672–c.1684	c.1696		1685 James II
			1689 Wm. & My.
			1694 William III
1702	1709	1716	
1703	1710	1717	1702 Anne
1704	1711	1718	1714 George I
1705	1712	1719	
1706	1713	1720	
1707	1714		
1708	1715		

				1735
	1721	𝕒	1728	1736
	1722	𝕓	1729	1737
	1723	𝕔	1730	1738
George I	1724	𝕕	1731	1739
1727 George II	1725	𝕖	1732	
	1726	𝕗	1733	Between 1721 and 1728, the shapes of date shields and lion passant marks often varied. The lion sometimes faced to the left.
𝕒	1727	𝕘	1734	

Date letters 1735–1739 shown: P, Q, R, S, T

			1747	H
	1740	A	1748	I
	1741	B	1749	K
	1742	C	1750	L
George II	1743	D	1751	M
	1744	E	1752	N
	1745	F	1753	O
A	1746	G	1754	P

Date letters 1755–1758: Q, R, S

88

1759	1775	1782	
1760–1768	1776	1783	
1769	1777	1784	
1770	1778	1785	George II
1771		1786	1760 George III
1772	1779	1787	
1773	1780	1788	
1774	1781	1789	
		1790	

1791	1799	1806	
1792		1807	
1793	1800	1808	
1794	1801	1809	George III
1795	1802	1810	
1796	1803	1811	
1797	1804	1812	
1798	1805	1813	
		1814	

Monarch	Year	Letter	Year	Letter	Year	Letter
George III	1815	A	1823	I	1831	R
	1816	B	1824	K	1832	S
	1817	C	1825	L	1833	T
1820 George IV	1818	D	1826	M	1834	U
1830 William IV	1819	E	1827	N	1835	W
1837 Victoria	1820	F	1828	O	1836	X
	1821	G	1829	P	1837	Y
	1822	H	1830	Q	1838	Z

Monarch	Year	Letter	Year	Letter	Year	Letter
Victoria	1839	A	1846	H	1855	Q
	1840	B	1847	I	1856	R
	1841	C	1848	J	1857	S
	1842	D	1849	K	1858	T
	1843	E	1850	L	1859	U
	1844	F	1851	M	1860	Y
	1845	G	1852	N	1861	W
			1853	O	1862	X
			1854	P	1863	Z

1864	ⓐ	1871	ⓗ	1879	ⓠ		
1865	ⓑ	1872	ⓘ	1880	ⓡ		
1866	ⓒ	1873	ⓚ	1881	ⓢ	Victoria	
1867	ⓓ	1874	ⓛ	1882	ⓣ		
1868	ⓔ	1875	ⓜ	1883	ⓤ		
1869	ⓕ	1876	ⓝ	In 1884, the Newcastle Assay Office closed.			
1870	ⓖ	1877	ⓞ				ⓐ
		1878	ⓟ				

91

Norwich

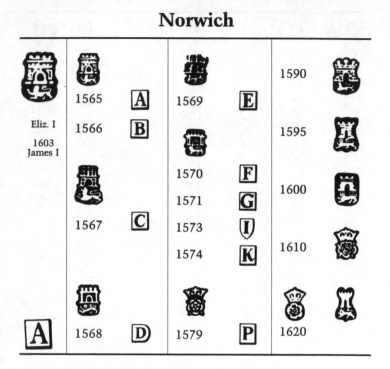

	1565	A	1569	E	1590	
Eliz. I	1566	B			1595	
1603 James I			1570	F		
	1567	C	1571	G	1600	
			1573	I		
			1574	K	1610	
A	1568	D	1579	P	1620	

		1630	G	1637	O	
With variations						James I
1624	A	1631	H	1638	P	1625 Charles I
1625	B	1632	I	1639	Q	
1626	C	1633	K	1640	R	
1627	D	1634	L	1641	S	
1628	E	1635	M	1642	T	
1629	F	1636	N	1643	V	A

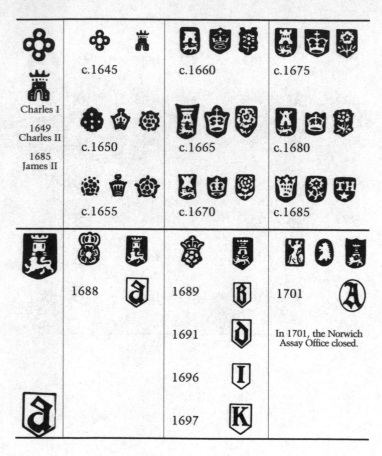

	c.1645	c.1660	c.1675
Charles I			
1649 Charles II	c.1650	c.1665	c.1680
1685 James II	c.1655	c.1670	c.1685
	1688	1689	1701
		1691	In 1701, the Norwich Assay Office closed.
		1696	
		1697	

Sheffield

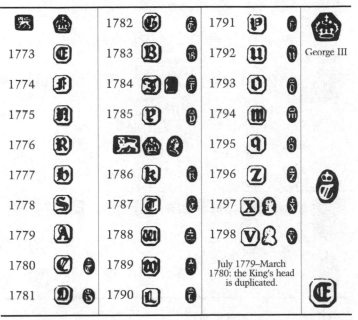

		1782	1791	
1773		**1783**	**1792**	George III
1774		**1784**	**1793**	
1775		**1785**	**1794**	
1776			**1795**	
1777		**1786**	**1796**	
1778		**1787**	**1797**	
1779		**1788**	**1798**	
1780		**1789**		
1781		**1790**	July 1779–March 1780: the King's head is duplicated.	

George III	🦁 👑 🧍	1807	S	Ŝ	1816	T	T
1820 George IV	1799 E	Ė	1808 P	P̂	1817	X	X̂
E	1800 N	N̂	1809 K	K̂	1818	I	Î
	1801 H	Ĥ	1810 L	L̂	1819	V	V̂
	1802 M	M̂	1811 C	Ĉ	1820	Q	Q̂
	1803 F	Ĥ	1812 D	D̂	1821	Y	Ŷ
	1804 G	Ĝ	1813 R	R̂		🦁 🧍 👑	
	1805 B	B̂	1814 W	Ŵ	1822	Z	Ẑ
Ŝ	1806 A	Â	1815 O	Ô	1823	U	Û

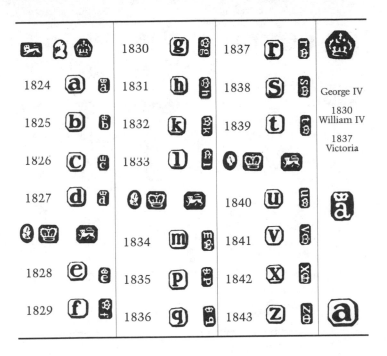

1824	1830	1837
1825	1831	1838	George IV
1826	1832	1839	1830 William IV
1827	1833		1837 Victoria
1828	1834	1840	
1829	1835	1841	
	1836	1842	
		1843	

Victoria	1844 **A**	1851 **H**	1860 **S**
	1845 **B**	1852 **I**	1861 **T**
	1846 **C**	1853 **K**	1862 **U**
	1847 **D**	1854 **L**	1863 **V**
	1848 **E**	1855 **M**	1864 **W**
	1849 **F**	1856 **N**	1865 **X**
	1850 **G**	1857 **O**	1866 **Y**
		1858 **P**	1867 **Z**
		1859 **R**	

🛡️ 🦌 💧		1876	J	1885	S	🛡️
1868	A	1877	K	1886	T	Victoria
1869	B	1878	L	1887	U	
1870	C	1879	M	1888	V	
1871	D	1880	N	1889	W	
1872	E	1881	O	🛡️ 🦌		
1873	F	1882	P	1890	X	
1874	G	1883	Q	1891	Y	
1875	H	1884	R	🛡️ 🦁		
				1892	Z	A

👑 (crown)	👑 (crown)	🦁 (lion)	1901	**i**	1910	**s**
Victoria	1893	**a**	1902	**k**	1911	**t**
1901 Ewd. VII	1894	**b**	1903	**l**	1912	**u**
1910 George V	1895	**c**	1904	**m**	1913	**v**
	1896	**d**	1905	**n**	👑 (crown)	🦁 (lion)
	1897	**e**	1906	**o**	1914	**w**
	1898	**f**	1907	**p**	1915	**x**
	1899	**g**	1908	**q**	1916	**y**
a	1900	**h**	1909	**r**	1917	**z**

		1926	**i**	1934	**r**	
1918	**a**	1927	**k**	1935	**s**	George V
1919	**b**	1928	**l**			1936 Ewd. VIII
1920	**c**	1929	**m**	1936	**t**	1936 George VI
1921	**d**	1930	**n**	1937	**u**	
1922	**e**	1931	**o**	1938	**v**	
1923	**f**	1932	**p**	1939	**w**	**a**
1924	**g**	1933	**q**	1940	**x**	
1925	**h**			1941	**y**	
				1942	**z**	

1936 George VI / 1952 Eliz. II	1943	A		1953	L		1964	W
	1944	B		1954	M		1965	X
	1945	C		1955	N		1966	Y
	1946	D		1956	O		1967	Z
	1947	E		1957	P			
	1948	F		1958	Q			
	1949	G		1959	R			
	1950	H		1960	S			
	1951	I		1961	T			
	1952	K		1962	U			
A				1963	V			

Eliz. II	1968	A	1971	D	1974	G
	1969	B	1972	E		
	1970	C	1973	F		

		1983	𝒥	1992	𝒮		
1975	𝒜	1984	𝒦	1993	𝒯	Eliz. II	
1976	ℬ	1985	ℒ	1994	𝒰		
1977	𝒞	1986	ℳ	1995	𝒱		
1978	𝒟	1987	𝒩	1996	𝒲		
1979	ℰ	1988	𝒪	1997	𝒳		
1980	ℱ	1989	𝒫	1998	𝒴		
1981	𝒢	1990	𝒬	1999	𝒵 2000		
1982	ℋ	1991	ℛ				
2000	ⓐ 2000					Eliz. II	
2001	ⓑ						
2002	ⓒ						
						ⓐ	

York

	During this period several variations of this town mark may be found.				

Eliz. I			1568	**K**	
	1562	**D**	1569	**L**	1575 **R**
	1564	**F**	1570	**M**	
			1572	**O**	1576 **S**
	1565	**G**	1573	**P**	1577 **T**
D	1566	**H**	1574	**Q**	1582 **Z**

	During this period several variations of this town mark may be found.				

					1596 **o**
	1583	**a**	1592	**k**	1597 **p**
	1584	**b**	1593	**l**	1598 **q**
	1587	**e**	1594	**m**	1599 **r**
a	1590	**h**	1595	**n**	1601 **t**
					1604 **x**

1607	1615	1624	
1608	1616	1625	
1609	1617	1626	
1610	1618	1627	
1611	1619	1628	
1612	1620	1629	
1613	1621	1630	
1614	1622		
	1623		
1631	1638	1650	Charles 1
1632	1639	1651	1649 Charles II
1633	1641	1652	
1634	1642	1653	
1635	1643	1654	
1636	1645	1655	
1637	1649	1656	

105

Charles II		1664	🄷	1673	🅡
		1665	🄹	1674	🅢
	1657	A	1666	🄺	1675	🅣
	1658	B	1667	🄻	1676	
	1659	C	1668	M	1677	🅥
	1660	D	1669	N	1678	🅦
	1661	E	1670	Ø	1679	🅧
	1662	F	1671	P	1680	🅨
A	1663	G	1672	Q	1681	Z
		1689	H		
	1682	A	1690	J	1696	P
	1683	B	1691	k	1697	Q
	1684	C	1692	L	1698	R
	1685	d	1693	M	1699	S
	1686	e	1694	N		
	1687	f	1695	O		
A	1688	G			

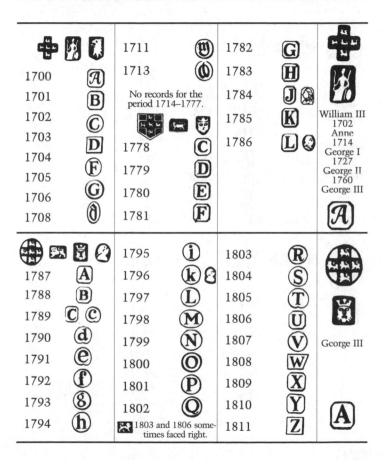

1700	1711	1782	William III 1702
1701	1713	1783	Anne 1714
1702	No records for the period 1714–1777.	1784	George I 1727
1703	1778	1785	George II 1760
1704	1779	1786	George III
1705	1780		
1706	1781		
1708			
1787	1795	1803	George III
1788	1796	1804	
1789	1797	1805	
1790	1798	1806	
1791	1799	1807	
1792	1800	1808	
1793	1801	1809	
1794	1802	1810	
	1803 and 1806 sometimes faced right.	1811	

107

George III	1812	a	1820	i	1829	s	
	1813	b	1821	k	1830	t	
1820 George IV	1814	c	1822	l	1831	u	
	1815	d	1823	m	1832	v	
1830 William IV	1816	e	1824	n	1833	w	
	1817	f	1825	o	1834	x	
	1818	g	1826	p	1835	y	
a	1819	h	1827	q	1836	z	
			1828	r			

Victoria	1837	A	1844	H	1852	Q
	1838	B	1845	I	1853	R
	1839	C	1846	K	1854	S
	1840	D	1847	L	1855	T
	1841	E	1848	M	1856	V
	1842	F	1849	N		
A	1843	G	1850	O		
			1851	P		

In 1857, the York Assay Office closed.

Makers' Marks

A

William Abdy
London
1784

Robert Abercromby
London
1739

1740

Stephen Adams
London
1813

Charles Aldridge & Henry Green
London
1775

Colline Allen
Aberdeen
1748

1748

George Angel
London
1850

1861

1875

John Angel & George Angel
London
1840

Joseph Angel & John Angel
London
1831

Joseph Angel
London
1811

1849

Peter Archambo
London
1720

1722

1739

Peter Archambo & Peter Meure
London
1749

B

John Backe
London
1700

1720

Thomas Bamford
London
1719

1720

1739

Joseph Barbitt
London
1703

1717

1739

Edward, John & William Barnard *London* 1846	
John Barnard *London* 1702	
1720	
1720	
James Le Bas *Dublin* 1810	
1819	
Hester Bateman *London* 1761	
1774	
1776	
1778	
1789	

Peter, Ann & William Bateman
London
1800

1800

Peter & Jonathan Bateman
London
1790

1790

Peter & William Bateman
London
1805

1805

William Bateman
London
1815

Harry Beathume
Edinburgh
1704

Joseph Bird
London
1697

1697

1724

Thomas Bolton *Dublin* 1701	
1701	
1706	
William Bond *Dublin* 1792	
George Boothby *London* 1720	
1720	
1739	
James Borthwick *Edinburgh* 1681	
Mathew Boulton *Birmingham* 1790	
Mathew Boulton & John Fothergill *Birmingham* 1773	

Thos Bradbury and Sons
Sheffield
1832

1867

1878

1885

1889

1892

Jonathan Bradley
London
1697

Robert Breading
Dublin
1800

1800

John Bridge
London
1823

1823

1823

Walter Brind
London
1748

1751

1751

1781

Robert Brook
Glasgow
1673

Alexander Brown
Dublin
1735

George Brydon
London
1720

1720

William Burwash
London
1802

1803

1813

William Burwash & Richard Sibley
London
1805

C

John Cafe
London
1742

1742

William Cafe
London
1757

Robert Calderwood
Dublin
1727

1760

William Charnelhouse
London
1703

John Chartier
London
1698

1723

1723

Henry Chawner
London
1786

1787

William Chawner
London
1819

1820

1823

1833

Francis Clarke
Birmingham
1836

Nicholas Clausen
London
1709

1720

Jonah Clifton
London
1703

1720

John Clifton *London* 1708	
Cocks & Bettridge *Birmingham* 1806	
Ebenezer Coker *London* 1739	
1745	
1751	
Lawrence Coles *London* 1697	
John Cooke *London* 1699	
Mathew Cooper *London* 1702	
1705	
1720	

Robert Cooper
London
1697

Thomas Corbet
London
1699

1699

Edward Cornock
London
1707

1723

Augustin Courtauld
London
1729

1739

Samuel Courtauld
London
1746

1751

Louisa & Samuel Courtauld
London
1777

Henry Cowper
London
1782

1787

Paul Crespin
London
1720

1720

1739

1740

1757

Joseph Creswick
Sheffield
1777

Thomas and James Creswick
Sheffield
1810

Thomas, James & Nathaniel Creswick
Sheffield
1862

1862

William Cripps
London
1743

1746

1751

John Crouch
London
1808

Francis Crump
London
1741

1745

1750

1756

W. & P. Cunningham
Edinburgh
c.1780

1790

1790

Louis Cuny
London
1703

D

Thomas Daniel
London
1744

1775

1783

William Davie
Edinburgh
1740

1740

William Dempster
Edinburgh
1742

William Denny
London
c.1697

William Denny & John Barro
London
1697

John Denziloe
London
1774

Isaac Dighton *London* 1697	
John Downes *London* 1697	
Nicholas Dumee *London* 1776	

E

John East *London* 1697	
John Eckford *London* 1698	
1720	
1725	
1725	
1739	

John Edwards
London
1697

1724

1724

1739

1753

Charles Eley
London
1825

William Eley & George Pierpont
London
1777

William Eley
London
1778

1785

1790

1795

William Eley
London
1795

1795

1825

1826

1826

William, Charles & Henry Eley
London
1824

Elkington, Mason & Co.
Sheffield
1859

William Elliott
London
1813

John Emes
London
1798

1802

Thomas Evans
London
1774

1779

1782

F

John Farnell
London
1714

1720

Thomas Farren
London
1707

1739

John Fawdery
London
1697

1720

William Fawdery *London* c.1697	
1720	
1720	
Edward Feline *London* 1720	
1720	
1739	
Fenton Brothers *Sheffield* 1860	
1875	
1883	
1888	
1891	
1896	

William Fleming
London
c.1697

Andrew Fogleburg & Stephen Gilbert
London
1780

1780

Thomas Folkingham
London
1706

1720

William Fordham
London
1706

1720

Charles Fox
London
1822

1823

1823

1823

Charles Fox
London
1823

1838

George Fox
London
1861

1869

1891

Charles Thomas and George Fox
London
1841

James Fraillon
London
1710

1722

William Frisby and Paul Storre
London
1792

G

Daniel Garnier
London
1697

Robert Garrard
London
1802

1818

1822

1847

Francis Garthorne
London
1697

George Garthorne
London
1697

Dougal Ged
Edinburgh
1734

Pierre Gillois
London
1754

1782

James Glen *Glasgow* 1743	
Elizabeth Godfrey *London* 1741	
John Goode *London* 1701	
Andrew Goodwin *Dublin* 1736	
1739	
Hugh Gordon *Edinburgh* 1744	
James Gould *London* 1722	
1722	
1732	
1739	
1747	
1748	

William Gould
London
1732

1734

1739

1748

1753

Robert Gray & Son
Glasgow
1819

David Green
London
1701

1720

Henry Greenway
London
1775

William Gwillim
London
1740

William Gwillim & Peter Castle
London
1744

H

Hamilton & Inches
Edinburgh
c.1880

John Hamilton
Dublin
1717

1720

Charles Hancock
London
1799

1814

Charles Frederick Hancock
London
1850

1850

1870

1870

John Hardman & Co.
Birmingham
1876

Peter Harrache *London* 1698	
1698	
Charles Hatfield *London* 1727	
1727	
1739	
Hawksworth Eyre & Co. *Sheffield* 1833	
1867	
1869	
1873	
1892	
1894	

Robert Hennell *London* 1773	R·H
1809	RH
1820	RH
1826	RH
1834 *(fourth generation)*	R·H
Robert & David Hennell *London* 1795 (third generation)	RH DH
Robert, David & Samuel Hennell *London* 1802	R H D·H S·H
Robert & Samuel Hennell *London* 1802	R·H S·H
Samuel Hennell *London* 1811	S·H
Samuel Hennell & John Terry *London* 1814	SH IT

Henry Herbert
London
1734

1735

1739

1739

1747

1747

Samuel Herbert
London
1747

Samuel Herbert & Co.
London
1750

John Hodson
London
1697

William Holmes & Nicholas Dumee
London
1773

William Holmes *London* 1776	**WH·**
Daniel Holy & Co. *Sheffield* 1776	**DH**
1778	**DH&C?**
Samuel Hood *London* 1697	**HO**
1720	**Ho**
Charles Hougham *London* 1773	**CH**
1785	**CH**
1786	**CH**
Francis Howden *Edinburgh* 1781	**FH**

I

Thomas Issod
London
1697

J

Joseph Jackson
Dublin
1799

John Jacob
London
1734

1739

1760

K

Charles Kandler
London
1727

1778

1778

Charles Kandler & James Murray
London
1727

1727

Charles Frederick Kandler
London
1735

1735

Frederick Kandler
London
1739

1758

Michael Keating
Dublin
1779

1792

1854

William Keats
London
c.1697

1697

1697

John Keith
Banff
1795

James Kerr
Edinburgh
1723

David King
Dublin
1706

1710

L

George Lambe
London
1713

Jonathan Lambe
London
c.1697

Paul de Lamerie
London
1712

1732

1739

John Lampfert
London
1748

1749

Louis Laroche
London
1725

1739

Samuel Laundrey & Jeffery Griffith
London
1731

Thomas Law
Sheffield
1773

1773

John Lawrence & Co.
Birmingham
1826

Samuel Lea
London
1711

1721

Lea & Clarke
Birmingham
1821

Ledsam, Vale and Wheeler
Birmingham
1824

George Lewis
London
1699

143

Charles Lias *London* 1837	**C L**
John, Henry & Charles Lias *London* 1830	**I L** **H L** **C L**
John & Henry Lias *London* 1837	**I·L** **H·L**
1839	**IL** **HL**
1843	**I L** **HL**
1845	**I·L** **H·L**
Henry John Lias & Henry John Lias *London* 1850	**H L** **H L**
1853	**H L** **H L**
1856	**H L** **H L**
Isaac Liger *London* 1704	**I L**
1720	**I L**

144

Mathew Linwood
Birmingham
1805

John Lloyd
Dublin
1771

Nathaniel Lock
London
1698

1698

1698

Mathew Lofthouse
London
1705

1721

Mary Lofthouse
London
1731

Seth Lofthouse
London
1697

Edward Lothian *Edinburgh* 1731	
Lothian and Robertson *Edinburgh* 1746	
James Luke *Glasgow* 1692	
William Lukin *London* 1699	
1699	
1725	
Benjamin Lumsden *Montrose* 1788	

M

Mackay and Chisholm *Edinburgh* c.1849	M&C
Jonathan Madden *London* 1702	MA
Mathew Madden *London* 1697	MA
Mappin Brothers *Sheffield* 1856	M&B
1859	MB
1867	MB
1867	EM JM
1878	EM JM
1883	CM
1885	FC CH
1889	F·C C·H

Mappin Brothers
Sheffield
1889

1893

1894

1894

John Newton Mappin
London
1882

1883

1884

1884

1885

1886

John Newton Mappin and George Webb
London
1866

1880

Jacob Margas *London* 1706	
1720	
Samuel Margas *London* 1714	
1720	
Marshall & Son *Edinburgh* c.1842	**M&S**
Colin McKenzie *Edinburgh* 1695	
Lewis Mettayer *London* 1700	
1720	
Nathaniel Mills *Birmingham* 1826	**NM**

Richard Mills
London
1755

1758

John Moore
Dublin
1729

1740

1745

Thomas Morse
London
1720

1720

Richard Morton
Sheffield
1773

1773

N

Robert Naughton
Inverness
1815

Anthony Nelme
London
1697

1722

Francis Nelme
London
1739

Samuel Neville
Dublin
1808

Newton & Son
Sheffield
1881

Henry Nutting & Robert Hennel
London
1808

O

Charles Overing
London
1697

P

Padley Parkin & Co.
Sheffield
1846

Padley Stanwell & Co.
Sheffield
1857

Mark Paillett
London
1698

Simon Pantin
London
1701

1717

1720

Thomas Parr
London
1697

Thomas Parr Jnr.
London
1717

1732

Thomas Parr Jnr.
London
1739

1739

John Parsons
Sheffield
1783

Humphrey Payne
London
1701

1701

c.1701

1739

Edmund Pearce
London
1704

1720

William Peaston
London
1745

William and Robert Peaston *London* 1796	
Samuel Pemberton *Birmingham* 1784	
Edward Penman *Edinburgh* 1706	
James Penman *Edinburgh* 1705	
Phipps & Edward Robinson *London* 1783	
Mathew Pickering *London* 1703	
Peze Pilleau *London* 1720	
1720	
1739	

John Pittar
Dublin
1751

1778

1813

William Pitts
London
1789

Pierre Platel
London
1699

Philip Platel
London
1737

John Pollock
London
1734

Thomas Powell
London
1756

1758

Joseph Preedy
London
1777

1800

John Pringle
Perth
1827

1827

Benjamin Pyne
London
c.1710

c.1720

R

Phillip Rainaud
London
1707

1720

John Rand
London
1703

Samuel Roberts
Sheffield
1773

Samuel Roberts Jnr. & George Cadman
Sheffield
1786

1786

Roberts & Belk
Sheffield
1864

1864

1892

1869

1879

Patrick Robertson
Edinburgh
1751

John (later Lord) Rollo
Edinburgh
1731

Phillip Rollos
London
1697

1697

1705

1720

Philip Rundell
London
1819

1819

1822

Abraham Russell
London
1702

S

John le Sage
London
1722

1739

1739

A. B. Savory
London
1826

1826

1826

1826

1826

1826

1836

John Schuppe
London
1753

John Scofield
London
1778

1787

Digby Scott & Benjamin Smith
London
1802

1803

William Scott *Banff* 1680	
James Seabrook *London* 1714	
1720	
Daniel Shaw *London* 1748	
William Shaw *London* 1727	
1728	
1739	
1745	
1748	
William Shaw & William Priest *London* 1749	
1750	

W. & G. Sissons
Sheffield
1858

Gabriel Sleath
London
1706

1706

1720

1739

Gabriel Sleath & Francis Crump
London
1753

Benjamin Smith
London
1807

Daniel Smith & Robert Sharp
London
1780

1780

1780

Edward Smith
Birmingham
1833

James Smith
London
1718

1720

1744

Stephen Smith
London
1865

1878

1880

Paul Storr
London
1799

1807

1808

1817

1834

John Sutton
London
1697

Thomas Sutton *London* 1711	
John Swift *London* 1739	
1739	
1757	
James Sympsone *Edinburgh* 1687	
1687	
Richard Syng *London* 1697	
1697	

T

Benjamin Tait
Dublin
1791

James Tait
Edinburgh
1704

Ann Tanqueray
London
1713

David Tanqueray
London
1713

1720

Joseph Taylor
Birmingham
1812

Samuel Taylor
London
1744

Taylor & Perry
Birmingham
1834

Thomas Tearle
London
1739

Edward Thomason
Birmingham
1817

1817

William Townsend
Dublin
1734

1734

1753

John Tuite
London
1739

William Tuite
London
1756

Joseph Turner
Birmingham
1838

U

George Unite *Birmingham* c.1838	**GU**
Archibald Ure *Edinburgh* 1717	**AU**

V

Ayme Videau *London* 1739	
Edward Vincent *London* 1739	

W

Edward Wakelin *London* 1747	
John Wakelin & William Taylor *London* 1776	
1777	

Joseph Walker *Dublin* 1701	
Samuel Walker *Dublin* 1738	
Thomas Walker *Dublin* 1723	
Walker Knowles & Co. *Sheffield* 1836	
Joseph Ward *London* 1697	
Samuel Wastell *London* 1701	
1701	
Mathew West *Dublin* 1776	
Gervais Wheeler *Birmingham* 1835	

Thomas Whipham
London
1737

1739

Thomas Whipham & Charles Wright
London
1757

Thomas Whipham & William Williams
London
1740

Fuller White
London
1744

1750

1758

John White
London
1719

1724

1730

George Wicke
London
1721

1721

1735

Starling Wilford
London
1717

1720

1729

David Willaume
London
1718

1718

1728

1728

1734

Richard Williams
Dublin
1761

1775

William Williamson
Dublin
1773

1747

Joseph Willmore
Birmingham
1806

Thomas Willmore
Birmingham
1789

1796

John Winter & Co.
Sheffield
1836

John Wirgman
London
1751

Edward Wood
London
1722

1722

1735

1740

Samuel Wood
London
1733

1737

1739

1754

William Woodard
London
1741

John Wren
London
1777

Charles Wright
London
1775

1780

Y

James Young *London* 1775	**I·Y**
John Young & Co. *Sheffield* 1779	IY Cº
1779	YG & H

PORCELAIN AND POTTERY

The marks on porcelain and pottery are not regulated in the way that those on precious metals have been for so many years. Not every piece of pottery has a mark at all and the same mark may be found on pieces from different dates, factories and even countries. Imitations are common and genuine marks may be blurred and difficult to identify. Nevertheless, marks on pottery and porcelain can add useful information provided that they are approached with some caution and, most importantly, they are seen in conjunction with the knowledge that can be gained from the piece itself. If you want to be able to identify items of pottery or porcelain, it is essential that you get to know something about the many styles and methods of manufacture that have appeared over the years. The pictorial glossary which follows (see pages 193–212) will provide valuable assistance in distinguishing one type of ware from another, especially if you spend time touching and handling individual pieces at every opportunity.

Porcelain

Porcelain is a translucent ware, usually white, which may be either of 'hard paste' or 'soft paste'. The original hard paste porcelain was first made in China and the earliest imports into Europe were as long ago as the fifteenth century. It is made from a mixture of china clay (kaolin) and china stone and fired at a very high temperature. Despite the popularity of porcelain, European manufacturers were not able to make it until the method was successfully reproduced at Meissen in the eighteenth century.

Soft paste porcelain contains an additional mixture of bone ash, steatite clay or some other substance, and is fired at a lower temperature. It is not easy to distinguish hard from soft paste porcelain without considerable experience in handling specimens of the two. On the whole, hard paste porcelain has a more glittery glaze and the material itself is stronger.

Pottery

Essentially, pottery is made of clay, but many substances have been added to give extra strength and many different types and styles of decoration and glazing have been used.

Earthenware is made of some kind of clay, is opaque and may be of any colour.

Creamware is an earthenware with a cream-coloured glaze which might be mistaken for porcelain except that the texture and outline of the pieces is less sharp.

Stoneware is a type of earthenware that has been vitrified at a high temperature and is often semi-translucent in its thinner parts. It is strong, with sand or flint being added to the clay mixture.

Delft is an earthenware with a fine, white, tin glaze, made in the seventeenth and eighteenth centuries.

Majolica is a highly decorated tin-glazed earthenware originally from Italy.

Faïence is another tin-glazed earthenware.

Types of Mark

As the illustrations on pages 179–92 show, there are hundreds of different marks to be found on pottery and porcelain ware. However, there are only five main methods of applying the marks.

175

Impressed marks are stamped into the body of the soft, unfired clay, and are almost impossible to fake.

Raised marks, as the name implies, stand above the surface as in the case of the early Chelsea 'raised anchor', applied in the form of a tiny pad of clay.

Incised marks are similar to impressed marks in being applied to the soft clay before firing, but they are scratched into the surface rather than stamped in.

Underglaze marks were printed or painted on to the surface of the ware by hand before the glaze was applied. Until 1850, these marks were applied only in blue; later, other colours were also used.

Overglaze marks were painted or printed on to the surface of a piece after the glaze had been fired. A relatively low temperature was required to fire them, and for this reason they are the easiest marks to fake.

Do Not Be Misled!

Manufacturers invented marks to enable their wares to be recognised, but they also copied marks from foreign originals, usually when the intention was to imitate or rival a particular style of Oriental or Continental decoration. Thus Worcester copies of Meissen carry the borrowed 'crossed swords' mark and pseudo-Chinese numerals were applied to wares decorated in the 'Japan' style. At Coalport, pieces decorated in the French manner were occasionally marked with the hunting horn of Chantilly. Moreover, when the little Lowestoft factory imitated Worcester porcelain decorated with underglaze blue, they often borrowed that factory's open crescent and, at second hand, its Meissen crossed swords.

Many early factories were haphazard in their use of marks and even at a later period, as in the case of Chamberlains at Worcester, it was common to mark only one piece of a service. Furthermore, a service was not made as a unit but in batches of cups, saucers, plates and so on, which were stored and taken from the shelves as needed. The result is that pieces from one service may have different marks.

Establishing Dates

Although, as we have seen, it is easy to be misled, there are some simple guidelines which will help to establish the date of a piece.

- Printed marks only appeared at the beginning of the nineteenth century.
- Pattern marks which include the name of the pattern were only used after 1810 and are often much later.
- The diamond-shaped registration mark was only used between 1842 and 1883 (see page 268).
- 'Rg No', meaning Registered Number, was used from January 1884 onwards.
- Marks incorporating the Royal Arms or the word 'Royal' are nineteenth century or later.
- The words 'Limited', 'Ltd' and 'Trademark' date from the early 1860s onwards.
- The word 'England' was only used from 1891.
- The words 'Made in England' have only been used in the twentieth century.

Visual Index

On the following pages you will find a visual index to the marks you may come across on pottery and porcelain. The marks have been divided into groups in order to help you to find the one you want. The first group is of marks containing initials, illustrated in alphabetical order. The second group is of marks containing numbers, in numerical order. The third group is of marks containing words, in alphabetical order, and this is followed by pictorial marks, grouped according to basic shape. Beside each mark is the number of the page on which you will find a full description of the manufacturer.

Marks Containing Initials

271	**A**	270	**B**	217	**BD**	218	👑D
232	**A**	232	**B**	217	**B**	218	👑D
232	**A**	240	**B**	217	**CD**	218	⚔D
232	**A**	232	**B**	273	**OC**	218	👑A
273	**B**	233	**BFD**	273	**C**	273	**D**
	◄B►	254	**BM**	270	**C**	244	**Y**
214	**B**	243	**(crest)**	217	**&**		**◄E►**
214	**B6**		**◄C►**	273	**C**	232	**E**
233	**B**	215	**C**		**◄D►**	232	**E**
233	**Bx**	255	**C**	216	**D**	270	**E**
273	**B**	234	**G**	216	**D**	231	**E**

179

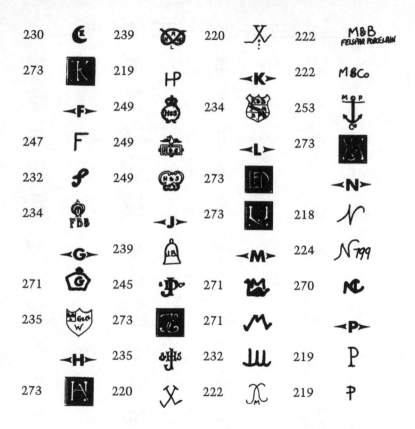

230		239		220		222	
273		219	HP		◄K►	222	M&Co
	◄F►	249		234		253	
247	F	249			◄L►	273	
232		249		273			◄N►
234	FBB		◄J►	273		218	
	◄G►	239			◄M►	224	N799
271		245		271		270	
235		273		271			◄P►
	◄H►	235		232		219	P
273		220		222		219	

Marks Containing Numerals

271	①	232	**2**	271	⑤	232	🖋
270	♈	271	③	232	🐚	232	⑧
271	🦢	271	♈	232	🦎	232	✒
271	②	271	🦢	271	⑥	253	🍖
271	♈	271	④	271	🦎	227	⬚⬚⬚⬚⬚
271	🦎	271	♈	232	🐛		
217	2	271	🦢	231	🖋		
225	2	225	4	271	⑦		

Marks Containing Words

245	245	◄E►
	245	D. J. EVANS & CO.
◄B►		
258	217 COALBROOKDALE	262 ◄F►
218	261	
257 BRAMELD	227 COPELAND	222 FENTON STONE WORKS
221 BRISTOL	227	252 FLIGHT
◄C►		233 Flight
262 CAMBRIA	260	
262 CAMBRIAN		233 Flight.
234 Chamberlains		233 Flight & Barr
234 CHAMBERLAIN	217 C Dale	◄G►
234	228 DILLWYN & CO.	222
	◄D►	

Pictorial Marks

232		149		230		217	
220		230		214		220	
225		230		214		262	
231		247		238		271	
231		213		239		271	
231		244		242		271	
213		216		240		271	
270		216		227		271	
218		244		255		271	

185

Square Devices

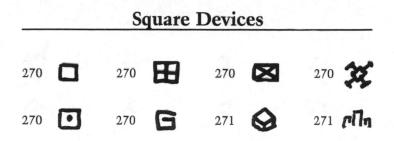

270   270   270   270

270   270   271   271

Angular Devices

Round Devices

270	270	270	232
232	271	232	213
270	271	232	213
270	217	232	
270	232	232	

Dotted Devices

232		222		232		232	
232		222		232		232	
232		270		232		232	
232		232		232		232	
270		270		232			
232		270		232			

190

Miscellaneous Devices

270		232		232		232	
270		232		232		271	
270		232		232		270	
232		232		232		270	
271		232		232		270	
232		232		232		271	
270		232		270		271	
271		232		271		271	
232		232		232		270	

Pictorial Glossary

Agate Wares

Whieldon tankard 6" high, c.1740–1750

Produced by a very specialised technique, the ware is usually associated with figures made by Astbury and tableware made by Whieldon between about 1740 and 1750. At best, Whieldon's ware was made in solid agate, as the tankard here illustrates. Pieces were made by layering clays of different colour, doubling and slicing. Later wares were given a surface agate effect by painting, combing or mingling together several colours of slip (liquid clay) on to an ordinary clay body. This later process was used in the 1770s and 1780s by Wedgwood and Bentley in the making of a wide range of marbled effects.

193

Belleek

Basket, 11" long, c.1860–1870

The best known of the ware associated with the Irish pottery in County Fermanagh is that which was fashioned in traditional marine shapes. A speciality, however, was openwork baskets of the kind illustrated whose form was probably introduced by Staffordshire workmen familiar with creamware shapes. The mark on this example is the standard printed mark of tower, dog and harp. It should be noted that this pottery is still in production and many of the patterns of the early period are still made.

Biscuit

Derby group, c.1795

Biscuit or *bisque* porcelain is a once-fired body without glaze. It is particularly suitable for figure making, since detail is not in any way obscured. Popular on the continent and in this country in the eighteenth century, it was used at Derby from about 1770 onwards. The best modeller was John James Spengler (or Spangler, son of the director of the Zurich porcelain factory), who was at Derby around 1790 to 1800. Biscuit figures were made during the early nineteenth century at several other factories, notably at Mintons. In about 1846, a new body called 'Parian' was invented by Copelands while attempting to find the secret of Derby biscuit. Parian was used thereafter in preference to ordinary biscuit because of its creamier colour.

195

Black Basalt

Wedgwood group,19" high, c.1770–1780

Basalt, or 'Egyptian black', was used at many factories for the making of tea wares from about 1760, and in a much improved form by Josiah Wedgwood from around 1773 to make classical figures, vases, plaques, etc. The improved stoneware body was smoother and a deeper black than that used, for example, by the Elers and Twyford, and it was ideally suited to fine modelling and engine turning. Wedgwood used it not only in its plain black form but also decorated it with unglazed enamels or relief ornamentation in red, and occasionally simulated the appearance of bronze by adding metallic powder to the mix.

Blue and White

Worcester plate, 7" diameter, c.1765–1770

Much of our earliest eighteenth-century porcelain was decorated in underglaze cobalt blue, to imitate and rival the 'Blue Nankin' imported from China. At first the decoration, usually in pseudo-Chinese style, was painted, but by about 1765 the process of overglaze printing, invented apparently at the same time at Worcester and Liverpool, had been adapted to underglaze blue use. Much of this printed ware was made at Worcester, Caughley, Liverpool, Lowestoft and other factories. This plate, marked with the hatched crescent, is printed in the centre with the familiar 'pine cone' pattern, while the border is painted. The appearance of this early blue and white is entirely different from that of the abundant blue-printed domestic wares made at Spodes and elsewhere during the period around 1780 to 1840.

Creamware

Leeds cruet, c.1780

Creamware was made as early as about 1720, when Astbury added white clay and flint to his bodies. By about 1750, it was widely produced throughout the Potteries, as being a vast improvement on any other cheaply produced domestic ware and indeed a dangerous rival to porcelain. Though its ultimate development was due to Wedgwood, who by 1767 had surpassed all his rivals in this sphere, Leeds creamware, made under the proprietorship of Hartley, Greens & Co., was also very fine between about 1780 and 1800. The piece illustrated is typical of the perforated ware in which each opening, like the Oriental 'rice grain' porcelain, was made with a separate punch and not, as was later done at Wedgwoods, by a multiple tool.

Delft

Lambeth posset pot, c.1700

Delft has a light, porous body covered with an opaque, white oxide-of-tin glaze upon which decoration may be painted in blue or polychrome. Its name is taken from the Dutch town of Delft, because its manufacture reached England from the Netherlands in the sixteenth century. In due course this settled into three main centres – London, Bristol and Liverpool. Most early delft was decorated in Chinese styles, in a dashing, often crude, manner, which was enforced by the absorbent nature of the glaze. Because the ware had comparatively little strength and, as may be seen in this illustration, the glaze was apt to chip easily, it was dropped for the making of domestic wares in favour of the cleaner, lighter, durable creamware.

Doulton Ware

Various Doulton styles, 1873, 1875 and 1876

The decorative stoneware made at Doulton's Art Pottery from 1871 onwards is notable for its fine design and the accomplished decoration for which students from the Lambeth School of Art were responsible. Each example bears the mark of the decorator as well as the factory mark and often the date of manufacture. Thus, the illustration shows, from left to right, light blue slip decoration on a white body by Hannah B. Barlow, 1876, incised decoration filled in with cobalt blue on a white slip background by the same artist, 1875, and carved decoration with light blue and brown colouring by Arthur B. Barlow, 1873.

Exotic Birds

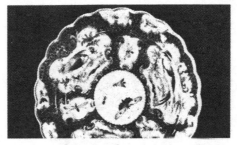

Worcester plate, 7¾" diameter, c.1768–1776

The so-called 'exotic birds' which are to be seen on many early English porcelains, had their origin in the *fantasie-vögell* invented in the 1770s at Meissen, and Worcester in particular. The painting of these incredible yet colourfully decorative creatures was developed to a remarkable extent. They were used in many different kinds of design, and are to be found in many distinctive styles, some being painted by London decorators and some by factory artists. The plate illustrated here, bearing the 'fretted square' mark, shows the characteristic Worcester combination of a scale-blue ground, upon which are gilt-scrolled reserves of birds and insects. It should be noted that this particular decorative style was often copied by Samson of Paris.

Martin Ware

Vase, 1887

The Martin brothers were early representatives of what we now call 'studio potters' – others were Bernard Moore and William de Morgan – who produced salt-glazed stonewares of outstanding quality first at Fulham and then later at Southall. One of the brothers, Walter, was trained at Doultons' pottery at Lambeth, and indeed there is a strong similarity between the wares made at Lambeth and those made by the Martins. Their pottery is best known for the jugs in the forms of grotesque, almost horrifying, animals and birds. The vase illustrated, bearing an incised pattern of fish and sea plants on a fawn ground, is representative of the more restrained kind of Martin ware, and bears the full, incised, written mark together with the numerals 8–87.

Mason's Ironstone China

Vases and jug, c.1813–1825

A very strong earthenware, patented by Charles James Mason in 1813, to meet the demand for showy, often gaudy, ware by those who could not afford fine porcelain. Of this new body, Mason made a wide range of dinner and dessert services, vases, jugs, and even fireplaces. The Chinese influence is usually present both in design and decoration. The Chinese landscapes of the pieces illustrated have transferred pink outline washed in with enamels, and while the vases are heavily gilded, the jug has yellow enamel instead of the gold, a common Mason practice. It should be noted that a striking variety of the ware has fine gilding, or gilding and thick enamels, applied upon a rich mazarine-blue ground, and that occasionally a piece may be found bearing panels of fine painting of landscapes, flowers or fruit.

Moulded Ware

Liverpool teapot, 8" high, c.1750–1770

Since so much pottery and porcelain was made in moulds, skilled modellers could not only fashion their own original designs, but were also able at will to copy silver shapes and the designs used at other factories. While some early factories, such as Worcester, made great use of moulded forms from the beginning, others such as New Hall confined their attention to shape alone, with no attempt to decorative detail. Once thought to have been made at Longton Hall, the type of teapot illustrated here, with its crisp moulding of palm trees and strawberry leaves, has now been credited to Liverpool.

Oriental Decoration

*Worcester vase
and cover, c.1770*

When European potters began to decorate on porcelain they were
obliged to rely upon Oriental sources for their designs – they were
venturing into unknown territory, with no past experience. Most
styles were imitations of the Chinese, often but not always
anglicised. Use was also made of the often simpler designs, mainly
in red, blue, green and gold, of the Japanese potter Kakiemon. Bow
porcelain in particular was so decorated, but this fine Worcester
vase, marked with an open crescent and made around 1770, is
painted with what Worcester called the 'old pheasant Japanese
pattern' reserved on a scale-blue ground, with the usual scrolling
in fine honey gold.

Powdered Blue

Bow plate, c.1755–1760

Amongst all the types of painting in underglaze blue on eighteenth-century English porcelain, powdered blue is particularly attractive. This ground colour, copied from the Chinese, was applied by blowing the dry pigment through a tube, closed at one end with gauze, over the moistened surface of the ware, thus giving the granulated appearance visible in the photograph. The reserves were of course masked during the process. The central reserve contains an exceedingly rare subject, in that the name of the factory responsible for its manufacture, Bow, is to be seen written on the base of the vase. It may be dated around 1755 to 1760. Powdered blue was also used at Worcester, Caughley and Lowestoft.

Pratt Ware

Bread plate, dated 1851

The name of F. & R. Pratt of Fenton is associated with a new way of printing in multicolours, each applied from a separate plate. This is seen not only on their well-known pot lids, but also upon dessert services, tea wares, mugs, jugs, etc. This kind of ware was shown at the 1851 Exhibition, for which event this bread plate was specially produced by Jesse Austin, the chief designer, after H. Warren's *Christ in the Cornfield*.

Pratt Ware

Jug, 8" high, c.1820

Another kind of popular Pratt ware takes the form of moulded jugs, such as this 'Parson and Clerk', made between about 1780 and 1800 by William Pratt of Lane Delph, father of Felix and Richard. The mark 'Pratt' is sometimes found impressed, but similar jugs were made elsewhere. The high-temperature-fired, coloured glazes Pratt used are quite distinctive.

Salt-glazed Ware

Staffordshire dish, c.1750–1760

By about 1720, Staffordshire potters had evolved a pottery which, by reason of its lightness, thinness, durability and delicacy, was a fair substitute for imported Chinese porcelain. This was a white stoneware, high-fired so as to become semi-vitreous, and glazed with salt thrown into the kiln at a temperature above 2,000°F to combine chemically with the silicate in the clays to form a durable sodium silicate glaze that has a characteristic, pitted appearance like orange peel. At a later date, after about 1740, the ware was often gaily enamelled, but plain white moulded examples such as this are most attractive.

Slipware

Pilgrim flask, mid-fourteenth century

Slipware is the earliest kind of earthenware that can be considered
to be characteristically English. It is so called because a creamy
mixture of clay and water, called 'slip', was used for its decoration.
Slip was either painted on in large areas, trailed in lines and dots
from a quill-spouted pot, or 'combed' into the surface of the ware.
Alternatively, as in this example, it was used sparingly and thinly
to impart colour interest. The piece illustrated is a rare pilgrim
bottle dating from about 1350, lead-glazed, with splashes of white
slip and richly applied foliate ornamentation.

Stone China

Spode plate, c.1810–1820

Stone china, as pioneered by Josiah Spode the Second, was the precursor of Mason's ironstone china, being first produced in 1805 and quickly copied throughout the Potteries, under various names. Although of hard, clean appearance, it is an earthenware whose smooth surface has been whitened by blueing. Spode was decorated with transferred patterns mostly in the Chinese style, though often translated into the English idiom. The outline was always printed in a colour suited to the washed-in enamels, in this case, sepia.

Stoneware

Fulham tankard, 8" high, c.1765

Compared with white salt-glazed stoneware, specimens of this kind, which was made at Fulham about 1760, may appear clumsy in the extreme. They comprise, however, an important class of English earthenware which was made in London, Nottingham and elsewhere from the seventeenth century onwards. The applied ornamentation suggests that the piece chosen for illustration was made for a bell-ringer whose initials B.H. it bears. As is usual with this kind of tankard, the colour ranges from brown to buff, and the characteristic 'orange peel' pitting of the salt glaze is clearly visible.

Porcelain Marks

Belleek Pottery

Belleek, Co. Fermanagh, Ireland. Founded 1863.

1. Impressed or printed, 1863–1880.
2. Impressed or printed, the standard mark 1863–1891. Continued in various forms. 'Co. Fermanagh' and 'Ireland' added c.1891.

Distinguished by a nacreous glaze often constrasted with the unglazed parts of the Parian style body. Tea wares (very thinly potted). Dessert and cabaret sets, figures, and ornamental wares often modelled after marine motifs. Great use of delicate shading in green or pink.

Bow China Works

Stratford, London, c.1747–c.1776.

1. & 2. Early incised marks.
3. Anchor and dagger mark, painted, c.1760–1776.
4. In underglaze blue, c.1760–1776.
5. & 6. Impressed marks of the 'repairer' Tebo, but also found on other porcelain.

Usually sensible durable wares, in contrast with those made at Chelsea, which catered for a more fashionable clientèle. Much painted underglaze blue decoration and use of Japanese Kakiemon designs and of the famille-rose enamels of pink, pale green, pale opaque blue and aubergine (purplish mauve). Good figures, at first crude and heavy, but neater after c.1754, when scrolled bases replaced plain ones.

Bristol ('hard paste' factory)

Founded by William Cookworthy c.1770, later Cookworthy and Richard Champion, closed 1781.

These painted marks are found in many forms, with different painters' numbers.

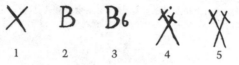

In common with Plymouth and New Hall, they were makers of true porcelain, resembling white glass, with a thin, colourless glaze and a pale grey translucency. Often recognisable by 'wreathing' (the marks of the potter's fingers as he worked at his wheel) inside bowls, jugs, mugs, etc.

Caughley (or Salopian) Works

Nr. Broseley, Shropshire. Proprietor Thomas Turner, and later John Rose & Co., 1775–1799.

1.–3.   Printed in underglaze blue on underglaze blue wares c.1775–1790.

4.   Printed in underglaze blue on underglaze blue wares c.1775–1790, and not to be confused with the Worcester crescent.

5.   Painted in underglaze blue on powder-blue wares c.1775–1790.

6. & 7. Impressed, usually in lower case letters c.1775–1790, and sometimes accompanied by underglaze blue marks.

1 2 3 4 5

6 7

Pronounced 'calf-ley', and until recently regarded as makers of rather inferior ware in the Worcester style. There has now been a wide reclassification of much of the porcelain made at the two factories, in the light of recent site excavations.

Chelsea Porcelain Works
Chelsea, London. c.1745–1769.

1. & 2. Incised c.1745–1750. Rarely with the year 1745.
3. The 'raised anchor' mark on a raised pad of clay c.1749–1752. The anchor sometimes in red.
4. Small red anchor of the 'red anchor' period c.1752–1756.
5. Rare early mark in underglaze blue c.1748–1750.
6. & 7. Anchor in gold of the 'gold anchor' period c.1756–1759, and sometimes found on Derby wares painted at Chelsea c.1769–1775.

N.B. A large blue anchor is very occasionally found on pieces painted in underglaze blue.

1 2 3 4

215

5   6   7

In its day, the English rival of Meissen and other Continental factories in the production of elegant porcelain. Fine figures made from an early date, often lovelier than the Continental originals from which they were copied, but in turn much imitated by Samson of Paris, whose versions usually bear gold anchor marks.

Chelsea–Derby

William Duesbury of Derby purchased the Chelsea factory in 1769, and porcelains were decorated at Chelsea until c.1784.

1.   In gold and, rarely, in red.
2. & 3. In gold.

1   2   3

Coalport Porcelain Works

Coalport, Shropshire, proprietors John Rose & Co., c.1795, and at Stoke-on-Trent c.1926 onwards.

1.–4. Painted in underglaze blue on all kinds of ware c.1810–1825.
5.   Impressed mark on flat wares c.1815–1825.
6.   The Meissen 'crossed swords' in underglaze blue c.1810–1825. Note that the same mark is found on Worcester and Lowestoft porcelains.
7.   In enamels or in gold c.1851–1861.
8.   In enamels or in gold c.1861–1875, the letters denoting Coalport, Swansea and Nantgarw. John Rose had purchased the stock, moulds, etc. of the Welsh factories c.1820–1822.
9.   An early painted mark, also found in circular form, c.1805–1815. Specimens may be seen in the Godden and V. & A. Collections.
10. The crown mark c.1881 onwards. 'England' was added c.1891, and 'Made in England' from c.1920. The date refers to the founding of the original earthenware manufactory at Caughley.

N.B. The names Coalport and Coalbrookdale are synonymous, and do not indicate that there were two factories.

Always of excellent quality, particularly after the purchase of the moulds and stock-in-trade of the Welsh factories, and the employment of Billingsley. Most early wares were unmarked, but the names and work of many of its Victorian artists, c.1840–1880, are known.

Derby Porcelain Works

The original works, founded c.1750, closed in 1848, and a new one was started in King Street by former employees whose names appear in the marks used – Locker & Co., Courtney, and Stevenson Sharp, c.1849–1863. The factory was taken over by Stevenson & Hancock c.1859. The marks of the modern Royal Crown Derby Porcelain Company Ltd., est. 1876, are self-explanatory.

1. Incised c.1770–1780, also occasionally in blue.
2. Painted c.1770–1782.
3. Standard painted mark, in puce, blue or black c.1782–1800, and in red c.1800–1825.
4. Rare painted mark c.1795.
5. Printed mark of the Bloor period c.1825–1840.
6. Printed mark of the Bloor period c.1820–1840.
7. Printed mark of the Bloor period c.1830–1848.
8. Painted mark of Stevenson & Hancock c.1861–1935.
9. Printed mark of the modern company c.1878–1890.

N.B. The standard mark c.1890 onwards is an elaboration of No. 9, with the words 'Royal Crown Derby' above the crown, and 'England' or, after c.1920, 'Made in England'.

The products of the Derby factories span the history of porcelain-making from c.1750 to the present day, and in addition to the decorative styles peculiar to Derby, almost every type of decoration was attempted, especially under Duesbury, with an eye to commercial success. When the Chelsea, Bow and Longton Hall concerns were taken over, the manufacture of many of their characteristic styles was continued. No contemporary factory employed a larger or more expert staff of specialist painters, who decorated not only everyday wares, but the beautiful cabinet specimens for which Duesbury's factory is famous.

Liverpool

The wares of many eighteenth-century potteries have not yet been fully classified, and are rarely marked, with the exception of porcelain made at the Herculaneum Pottery, c.1793–1841.

1. & 2. Painted in enamels or in gold, probably by Seth or James Pennington c.1760–1780.
3.   Painted, and probably a Pennington mark, c.1760–1780.
4. & 5 Impressed or printed c.1796–1833.
6.   Impressed or printed c.1833–1836. The 'Liver Bird' mark is found in many forms.
7.   Impressed or printed c.1796–1833.

N.B. The full name of the factory – Herculaneum Pottery – was probably used, impressed, from about 1822.

It should be remembered that because a Worcester potter named Podmore went to Liverpool to join Richard Chaffers in 1755, to introduce the kind of steatite porcelain made at Worcester, there is often a marked similarity between some Liverpool and Worcester of the 'blue and white' variety.

219

Longton Hall Works
Founded by William Littler at Longton Hall, Staffordshire; c.1749–1760.
Few pieces are marked, but the marks illustrated are occasionally found on early wares painted in underglaze blue.

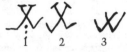

It is interesting to reflect that as far as we know, this was the only porcelain-making factory in the great potting centre of Staffordshire. Littler is best known as the inventor of the distinctive, vivid ground colour called 'Littler's blue', which he first used upon earthenware before venturing into porcelain making.

Lowestoft Porcelain Works
Lowestoft, Suffolk, c.1757–1802.
1. & 2. Copies of the Worcester crescent and Meissen crossed swords marks, in underglaze blue, on blue-and-white wares, c.1775–1790.
3. & 5. Examples of artists' marks, in underglaze blue, on blue-and-white wares c.1760–1775, usually painted near or inside the foot rim.

This small factory made mostly domestic wares, often of toy-like quality, simply decorated in underglaze blue painting or printing, or enamelled. At risk of repetition, it must be stressed that the factory was not responsible for the so-called 'Chinese Lowestoft' which was made in China for export to Europe. A great deal of ware has underglaze blue patterns similar to those used at Worcester and Caughley, and is often marked with the Worcester crescent or crossed swords.

Lund's Bristol

(Soft paste factory)

Redcliffe Backs factory c.1748–1751, owned by Benjamin Lund, and taken over by the Worcester proprietors.

The mark illustrated, in relief, is very rarely found upon moulded wares, and may be coupled with the equally rare relief mark 'Wigornia' on cream jugs and sauce boats made at the Worcester factory at the time of the take-over.

BRISTOL

Not to be confused with the 'hard paste' factory. It is most difficult to distinguish between Lund's Bristol (sometimes referred to as Redcliffe Backs) and very early Worcester, though the typical enamelled decoration found on some of it, of Oriental derivation, is recognisable by its jewel-like, dainty quality.

Minton

Stoke-on-Trent, Staffordshire, est. 1793.

1. Painted mark on porcelains made c.1800–1830, with or without a pattern number below.
2. Incised or impressed on early Parian figures c.1845–1850, sometimes with the year cypher.
3. & 4 Examples of printed marks indicating the several partnerships, c.g. Minton c.1822–1836, Minton & Boyle 1836–1841, Minton & Co. 1841–1873, and Minton & Hollins c.1845–1878. Cf. Nos. 6.–8.
5. The 'ermine' mark, painted, from c.1850 onwards, with or without the letter M.

6.–8.   Examples of the numerous printed marks which incorporate an indication of the partnership (and period) and, sometimes, a pattern name.

9. & 10. Printed marks of the 1860s.

11.   Standard printed 'globe' mark c.1863–1872. A crown was added c.1873, and an S to the word 'Minton'. In 1891 'England' was added below, and 'Made in England' c.1902. *See* Year Cyphers, page 270.

Naturally enough, early output consisted mostly of good-quality transfer-printed earthenwares, and in the early nineteenth century the factory gained a high reputation largely due to the work of well-known painters, some of them from Derby. Among the wares for which the factory is renowned are white Parian figures, *pâte-sur-pâte* decoration on tinted grounds, fine almost eggshell porcelain and majolica wares.

Nantgarw China Works
Nantgarw, Glamorgan, c.1813–1814 and 1817–1822.

1. Impressed mark 1813–1822. The C.W. (for 'china works') is sometimes omitted, as is the space between the two parts of the word.
2. Painted written mark c.1813–1822. The word may also be stencilled, in upper case letters, but cannot always be relied upon as authentic.

NANT GARW
C.W.

1

Nantgarw

2

The factory, with Swansea, was at once the glory and the downfall of the perfectionist William Billingsley. His 'soft paste' body was incomparably lovely and wonderfully decorated, but ruinously expensive to produce. Because he left Wales to go to Coalport, there is a real danger of mistaking a superlative piece of Coalport porcelain for a piece of Swansea or Nantgarw, and the collector has to learn the details of true Welsh shapes and artists' characteristic styles, and to remember that the clinching Nantgarw mark, impressed and impossible to forge, is often practically obscured by glaze.

New Hall Porcelain Works
Shelton, Hanley, Staffordshire, 1781–1835.

1. Painted pattern numbers usually in red or more rarely in black, on 'hard paste' wares c.1781–1812. Pattern numbers appear commonly without the N.
2. Printed mark on bone china c.1812–1835.

1   2

Much New Hall porcelain was once called 'Cottage Bristol', and, in fact, the Bristol hard paste factory was taken over by a company of Staffordshire potters in 1781. From the outset, apparently, after production began in the New Hall works, the decoration used was unlike anything done at Bristol being slight and crude and applied to an inferior, greyer paste. The bone-ash paste used later is much whiter and more whitely translucent. Although most New Hall decoration is inferior, the factory was occasionally able to produce a really elaborate, well-painted pattern, with gilding of high quality, black-printing of the batt variety, and very occasionally printing in underglaze blue. The collector very quickly learns the distinctive moulded shapes of tea wares in particular.

Pinxton Works

Pinxton, Derbyshire, c.1796–1813.

1.–3. Though Pinxton porcelain is rarely marked, these painted marks are sometimes seen. The P is sometimes found without a pattern number. After William Billingsley left the concern c.1799, his partner John Coke used the crescent and star mark, together with various arrow symbols, until c.1806.

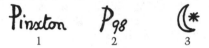

It may be supposed that here William Billingsley was first able to put his formulae to practical test, but in the more usual absence of marks the wares he made there are difficult to identify.

Plymouth Porcelain Works

Plymouth, Devon, under William Cookworthy, 1768–1770.

1. & 2. Painted 'tin symbol' marks in underglaze blue or enamels c.1768–1770. Also to be found on Samson imitations.

3. Impressed mark of the 'repairer' Tebo, found also on Bristol, Bow and Worcester wares.

See the notes under Bristol, because William Cookworthy moved from Plymouth to Bristol in 1770, and in 1773 left the business to his partner Richard Champion.

Rockingham Works
Near Swinton, Yorkshire, c.1745–1842.

Porcelain was not made here until c.1826, and thereafter the standard 'griffin' mark was used, at first in red until 1830, and then in puce, with various alterations to the wording beneath. Thus: 'Royal Rockingham Works' instead of 'Rockingham Works' and/or 'China Manufacturers to the King' c.1830–1842, and 'Manufacturers to the Queen' c.1837 on. Very rarely an impressed 'Rockingham Works, Brameld' or 'Rockingham Brameld' is seen on porcelain c.1826–1830.

So much Rockingham porcelain is so lavishly and expensively decorated that the factory could not have survived without the patronage of Earl Fitzwilliam. Unmarked Staffordshire porcelain is often called 'Rockingham', which is one reason why pieces bearing the 'griffin' mark are held in high regard.

Spode
Stoke-on-Trent, Staffordshire. Josiah Spode c.1784–1833, Copeland & Garrett 1833–1847, W. T. Copeland & Sons Ltd., 1847 to the present day.

1. Early workman's mark, painted in gold c.1790–1805.
2. A rare impressed mark on early wares c.1784–1805, and in printed form c.1805 onwards.
3. Written mark, usually in red, followed by a pattern number, c.1790–1820.

4. Printed in several styles, in puce or black on felspar porcelains c.1815–1827.
5. Impressed c.1784–1805.
6. Printed c.1847–1851, and with the Cs elaborated 1851–1885.
7. Printed 1875–1890.
8. One of the many self-explanatory printed marks of the period c.1833–1847.

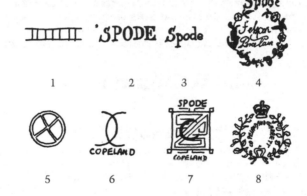

Throughout its life, the Spode factory, under any management, has never made anything of poor quality, and hardly any style of decoration has not been attempted. The collector is well advised to visit the collections on view at the Stoke factory.

Swansea

Swansea, Wales, 1814–1822.

1. Impressed, written or printed 1814–1822. In the impressed form, may be accompanied by a trident or two crossed tridents to indicate use of the 'trident paste'.
2. Impressed, sometimes with the word 'Swansea', c.1814–1817.
3. Painted 1814–22.

N.B. No. 1 is suspect in printed form, because the copper plates used to produce it became the property of the Coalport concern in 1822, and it is possible that they may well have been used there to mark the particularly fine porcelain made to Billingsley's recipes.

SWANSEA DILLWYN & CO.

1   2

Swansea

3

Much Swansea may be approximately dated by the kind of paste used, since Billingsley was obliged to make repeated efforts to save expense owing to kiln losses. Thus, in about 1816 the 'duck egg' paste, greenly translucent, was introduced, to be followed shortly afterwards by the still cheaper 'trident body', which did not please the London china dealers.

Josiah Wedgwood & Sons Ltd
Burslem c.1759, Etruria c.1769, Barlaston 1940.
1. Printed, very small, in red, blue or gold on bone china c.1812–1822.
2. Printed mark of the 'Portland vase' from c.1878. 'England' added below from 1891. A similar mark, but with the body of the vase left white, and with three stars beneath it, was used from c.1900. The words 'bone china' were added c.1920 and in 1962 the body of the vase was again filled in.

1   2

Josiah Wedgwood was a perfectionist, and from the beginning the name of Wedgwood has always been synonymous with quality, so that while many Staffordshire potters imitated, for example, his jasper and creamware, their products were for the most part of poorer quality.

Worcester

For convenience sake, the marks of all the various factories and companies in Worcester are placed together. Their dates are as follows:

THE MAIN FACTORY, c.1751–1840.
    First (or Dr. Wall) Period, 1751–1783.
    Davis/Flight or Middle Period, 1776–1793.
    Barr and Flight & Barr Period, 1792–1807.
    Barr Flight & Barr Period, 1807–1813.
    Flight Barr & Barr Period, 1813–1840.
CHAMBERLAINS & CO., c.1786–1852.
KERR & BINNS, 1852–1862.
GRAINGERS, c.1812–1902.
HADLEYS, 1896–1905.
LOCKES, 1895–1904.
WORCESTER ROYAL PORCELAIN CO., 1862 to present day.

WORCESTER MAIN FACTORY
First Period, c.1751–1783.
1.–4. Crescent marks c.1755–1790, in underglaze blue. 1. Open painted crescent found on wares painted in underglaze blue, or may rarely be found on enamelled wares, in gold or enamel.
2.–4. Printed, on wares in underglaze blue. Several other capital letters are found inside the crescent, which may also be found, rarely, in the shape of a face. Continued into the Davis/Flight period.

    1   2   3   4

5.   The fretted square, painted in underglaze blue c.1755–1770 on wares painted in underglaze blue, in several similar forms. Rarely accompanied by the crescent.

6.–9.   Painted or printed, according to whether the piece is painted or printed in underglaze blue, c.1755–1770.

10. & 11. Pseudo-Chinese marks painted in underglaze blue, many variations, c.1753–1770.

12.–14.   The Meissen 'crossed swords', painted in underglaze blue, usually found on wares painted in the Meissen style, c.1760–1770, but also found on pieces printed overglaze in puce enamel.

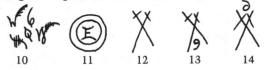

15.–17.   On pieces printed in overglaze enamel. The RH refers to the engraver and printer Robert Hancock, and the anchor is the rebus of Richard Holdship, a former proprietor of the factory.

231

18. Examples of numbers disguised as Chinese characters, and so known as 'disguised numerals', found on wares made c.1775–90, printed in underglaze blue on certain types of blue-printed wares formerly attributed to the Caughley factory.

18

19. Examples of workmen's or painters' marks painted on early underglaze blue-painted wares c.1751–65.

19

Davis/Flight period, 1783–1793.

20. Painted in blue, 1783–1788. A crescent alone, smaller than that used during the First Period, is also found.
21. A crown was added after the King's visit in 1788.
22. Found in various forms, painted in blue.

20   21   22

Barr and Flight & Barr period, c.1793–1807.

23. Incised, usually on tea-wares.
24. Written mark found in various forms. Also, several self-explanatory painted or printed marks.

23   24

Barr and Flight & Barr period, c.1807–1813.

25. Impressed, often accompanied by self-explanatory written or printed marks, sometimes with London addresses and Royal warrant.

25

Flight Barr & Barr period, c.1813–1840.
26. Impressed, and also as above.

CHAMBERLAINS, c.1786–1852
27. Early mark, c.1786–1810, found in many forms.

Chamberlains
27

Between c.1811 and 1840, many self-explanatory printed and written marks were used, some with London addresses, Royal warrants and crowns. Note that the words 'Regent China' denote a special body or paste used for expensive wares, c.1811–1820.

28. Impressed or printed, with or without 'Worcester', c.1847–1850.
29. Printed, c.1850–1852.

CHAMBERLAINS
28

29

KERR & BINNS, 1852–1862.
30. Printed or impressed. The crown added in 1862.
31. Shield mark c.1854–1862. The last two numerals of the year in the central bar, the artist's initials or signature in the bottom left-hand corner.

30

31

GRAINGERS, c.1812–1902.
Grainger, Lee & Co. c.1812–c.1839, then George Grainger & Co. c.1839–1902.
32. In several painted or printed forms.
33. Painted or printed in several forms, c.1812–1839.
34. Printed or impressed, c.1870 1889.

32   33   34

The same form of mark with 'Royal China Works' above and 'Worcester' below, was used c.1889–1902, and the word 'England' was added from 1891, when date letters were also added below, commencing with A.

HADLEYS, 1896–1905.
35. Incised or impressed on pieces modelled by James Hadley for the Worcester Royal Porcelain Company, c.1875–1894.
36. Printed or impressed, 1896–97.
37. Printed, Aug. 1902–June 30th, 1905.

35   36   37

Various other self-explanatory marks also used.

LOCKES, 1895–1904.
Founded by Edward Locke in the Shrub Hill Works, to make porcelain in the Royal Worcester style, and closed after a law action with the Royal Worcester company.
38. Printed mark, c.1895–1900.

38

WORCESTER ROYAL PORCELAIN COMPANY, 1862–present day.
The Flight Barr and Barr concern amalgamated with Chamberlains in 1840, and in 1852 reorganisation resulted in the foundation of a new company known as Kerr and Binns. When Kerr retired in 1862, the modern W.R.P.c.was formed. Note that Graingers were taken over in 1889 and Hadleys in 1905.

The Standard Mark

1862–1875. The standard Kerr and Binns mark (30.) was taken over, with an open crown above and a C in the centre instead of a crescent. Two numerals below denote the last two numerals of the year, and from 1867 a system of date letters was used, as follows:

A 1867	G 1872	M 1877	T 1882	Y 1887
B 1868	H 1873	N 1878	U 1883	Z 1888
C 1869	I 1874	P 1879	V 1884	O 1889
D 1870	K 1875	R 1880	W 1885	a 1890
E 1871	L 1876	S 1881	X 1886	

1876–1891. The same mark, but with a crescent replacing the C in the centre, and the crown filled in. Year letters commencing with 'a' for 1890, as above. This mark is also found in impressed form, without year letters.

1891 onwards. The same mark, with 'Royal Worcester, England' added. 'Made in England' denotes a twentieth-century origin.

A complicated system of arrangements of dots to denote year of manufacture was adopted from 1892, which may be referred to in G. A. Godden's *Encyclopaedia of British Pottery and Porcelain Marks*.

The standard mark has been revised from time to time, but is always self-explanatory.

Much of the early ware is unmarked, and even later, at Chamberlains and at Flights, the only mark on a service may be inside a teapot lid, sucrier cover, or beneath a single dish of a dinner or dessert service. The earliest 'blue and white' may bear either a workman's mark or a crescent, W or fretted square. With few exceptions, it is unusual to find a mark on First Period enamelled pieces that have no underglaze blue in their decoration, probably because the painter who applied the underglaze blue could conveniently also apply the mark in the same colour.

Pottery Marks

William Adams & Sons (Potters) Ltd

This concern, also known under several earlier titles, is perhaps the best known of the many Adams firms working in the Potteries during the eighteenth and nineteenth centuries. Founded c.1769.

1. Impressed, 1787–1805 on Jasper wares, 1800–1864 on earthenwares, with '& Co.' 1769–1800. Also on Parian figures 1845–1864.
2. Printed, from 1896 onwards.
3. Printed, with pattern name, 1819–1864. The initials below are found as a part of many other printed marks.
4. Printed mark on wares made for the American market c.1830–1850.

The finest Adams product is perhaps the blue jasper ware, violet-toned, and often less frigidly modelled than the Wedgwood variety which it imitated. It should be remembered that William Adams was a friend and favourite pupil of Wedgwood and a modeller of exceptional merit.

Edward Asbury & Co.
Longton, 1875–1925.
Printed mark 1875–1925.
Also found with the names 'Asbury' and 'Longton'.

H. Aynsley & Co. Ltd
Longton. 1873 onwards.
An example of the Staffordshire Knot mark used by many potters, usually with distinguishing initials similarly arranged, and with 'England' added from 1891 onwards.

Another Aynsley, named John, had a pottery in Longton from about 1864, making mostly porcelain but also lustre wares, bearing self-explanatory marks incorporating only the surname.

J. & M. P. Bell & Co. Ltd
Glasgow Pottery, 1842–1928.
1. & 2. Impressed or printed, with the addition of 'Ltd' or 'Ld'
    from 1881.

1   2

Belle Vue Pottery
Hull. Various proprietors from c.1802.
The 'two bells' mark, printed or impressed, c.1826–1841.

The original partnership was between Jeremiah and James Smith and Job Ridgway, until 1804 when Ridgway retired. The chief productions were domestic earthenware, green-glazed and blue-printed ware.

Bishop & Stonier Ltd
Hanley. 1891–1939. Formerly Powell, Bishop & Stonier.
Printed mark 1880–1936, after which date it was impressed. The initials B & S were also used in printed or impressed form, and there are several later (after c.1899) self-explanatory printed marks.

Booths Limited
Tunstall, 1891–1948.
Printed mark found on earthenware reproductions of First Period Worcester 'blue and white' porcelains. The fretted square of the same factory is also sometimes found. Enamelled reproductions are not commonly marked.

Booth reproductions are remarkably accurate as regards decoration, but are betrayed by their natural opacity, and, in the case of larger pieces such as openwork baskets in the enamelled Worcester style, by creaminess of paste and lightness of weight.

Bristol. Pountney & Co. Ltd
c.1849 onwards.
1. & 2. 1849–1889, and other marks incorporating initials or names.
3. 1884 on pieces specially glazed. The numerals below indicate month and year of manufacture. 'Ltd.' added after 1889.

P. & CO. POUNTNEY & CO. BRISTOL + 2/84

1 2 3

Creamware was first made in Bristol in about 1786, by Joseph Ring, who engaged potters from Shelton in the Potteries. Notable flower painters were William Fifield (1777–1857) and his son John, who continued to work with the Pountneys. Many pieces, brightly painted by them for Pountney and Allies, including distinctive small barrels, bear the name and date of the person for whom they were made.

Bristol. Pountney & Allies

c.1816–1835.
1. & 2. Printed, impressed or painted, c.1816–1835.
3.   Impressed, c.1816–1835.
4.   Printed in blue, c.1825.
5.   Impressed, 1816–1835.
6.   Printed in blue, 1830.

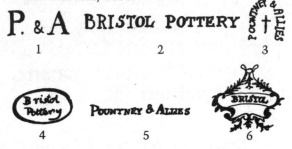

Britannia Pottery Co. Ltd

Glasgow, formerly Cochran & Fleming, 1896–1935.
Several forms of the printed seated Britannia mark, side-face or full-face, 1896–1920. Later forms have self-explanatory lettering.

There were in fact many late nineteenth-century potteries in Glasgow, all making the usual ironstones, creamware, stoneware and general domestic ware of the period.

Brown Westhead, Moore & Co.

Hanley, 1862–1904.
Printed mark, 1862 onwards. The initials, or the name in full, are found in various printed or impressed marks, sometimes with a pattern name. The word 'cauldron' appears in marks used c.1890.

They were the successors, after many partnerships, to the Ridgways – Job, John and William – who began business in 1802. W. Moore had been assistant to John Ridgway. The earthenwares, majolica, and Parian wares won the highest awards at many exhibitions throughout the world, being, in the words of J. F. Blacker, 'peculiarly good, hard, compact and durable, and the patterns chaste and effective'. Note that old Cauldron ware was marked with such marks as 'J. Ridgway', 'Ridgway & Sons' and 'John Ridgway & Co.'

Davenport

Longport, c.1793–1887.
1. & 2. Impressed, the name sometimes accompanied by an anchor. Lower case letters 1793–1810, upper case letters after 1805.
3. Printed on stone china, c.1805–1820.
4. Printed, c.1795, sometimes with 'Longport' instead of 'Davenport'. A later version was used up to about 1860, sometimes with the last two numerals of the year on either side of the anchor.
5. Impressed, on wares of all periods. Many other Davenport marks are self-explanatory.

1 2 3 4 5

John Davenport was an artistic potter, and is better known for his porcelain, which bears similar marks to those reproduced here. His blue-printed earthenwares are particularly fine, with perforated rims to plates and dishes, and he made stone china in the Mason style, as, for example, his octagonal jugs. Decoration is usually strong in colour, with occasional fine gilding, and some excellent painting of fruit was done, probably by Steele of Derby.

William de Morgan
Chelsea, Fulham, etc. London, c.1872–1907.
1. An example of the several name marks used c.1882 onwards. '& Co.' added after 1888.
2. Impressed or painted, 1882 onwards.

1 2

William de Morgan may be classed with Bernard Moore and W. Howson Taylor of 'Ruskin' fame as a studio potter who was inspired by the brilliant strength of colour of ancient Continental or Oriental wares, in de Morgan's case by the fine lustre effects on old Majolica and the intense blues of old Persian wares.

J. Dimmock & Co.
Hanley, 1862–1904.
1. Printed monogram mark, 1862–1878; sometimes the same initials are found with pattern names.
2.–4. Printed, c.1878–1904. From c.1878 the name of the new proprietor D. D. Cliff was used in many printed marks.

1   2   3   4

This firm originated in about 1816, when the son of Wedgwood's modeller, Hackwood, entered into partnership with John Dimmock to make earthenware.

Don Pottery
Swinton, Yorkshire, 1790–1893.
1. Impressed or painted c.1790–1830.
2. Impressed or painted, 1820–1834. Another version bears the words 'Green Don Pottery'.

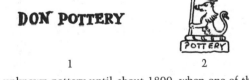

DON POTTERY

1   2

An almost unknown pottery until about 1800, when one of the brothers Green, of Leeds, became owner, so that many of the finest pieces made at Swinton were in fact of Leeds design.

Doulton & Co. Ltd
Lambeth and Burslem, c.1858–1956. The Lambeth works closed in 1956, while the Burslem works continued.

1. Impressed, c.1858 onwards. The same words are sometimes found impressed in an oval or, rarely, in a circle, with the year of manufacture between them.
2. & 7. Painted or impressed, c.1882–1902, with 'England' after 1891.
3. Impressed or printed, c.1887–1900.
4. Impressed, c.1881–1912, with 'England' after 1891.
5. Impressed or printed, c.1872 onwards.
6. Impressed, c.1888–1898.
8. The standard impressed Doulton mark, found in several forms from c.1902 onwards. 'Made in England' added in 1891.

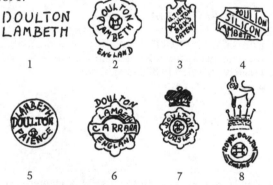

The revival of artistic stoneware was begun by Henry Doulton, the intention being to make domestic vessels as ornamental as the old Flemish ware. Actually a stoneware works was founded by John Doulton at

Vauxhall in 1815, afterwards being carried on by Doulton and Watts before being transferred to High Street, Lambeth, some years later. At the 1851 Exhibition the Lambeth terracotta wares were highly commended, but it was some 20 years later that the use of *sgraffito* (scratched) designs typical of Doulton ware were developed, while different coloured bodies were gradually introduced. Nineteenth-century Doulton ware may be divided roughly into the following classes: salt-glazed stoneware, usually simply called 'Doulton ware'; chiné ware (faïence either salt- or lead-glazed); silicon ware, which is vitrified stoneware without a salt glaze, but making use of coloured clays; Carrara ware which is covered with a transparent crystalline enamel; marqueterie ware made of marbled clays in chequered designs; Lambeth faïence which is a terracotta or biscuit body bearing underglaze painting, and glazed faïence mostly used for larger vases, architectural decoration and tiles. A considerable number of skilled artists were employed to decorate these wares, notably including the Barlow sisters and George Tinworth, whose work is usually signed with their monograms.

Thomas Fell & Co. Ltd

St Peter's Pottery, Newcastle-upon-Tyne, 1817–1890.
Impressed marks, 1817–1830. Between 1830 and 1890, initials or Christian name initial and full surname were impressed or printed in several forms, '& Co.' being added later.

A large group of potteries were situated on the rivers Tyne, Wear and Tees, mostly at Newcastle and Sunderland, and their wares had a predominantly nautical flavour, carried out in washed-in black transfer, often with pink lustre ornamentation. This can be seen in the well-known 'Wear Bridge' jugs, bowls and mugs made by Dixon & Co. of Sunderland. Most of these potters, including Fell, marked some of their products with name marks.

Gildea & Walker
Burslem, 1881–1885.
The mark first used by predecessors Bates Elliott & Co. c.1870 but without the words 'trademark', and afterwards, c.1885–1888, within a double circle, by successors James Gildea. The figure of the potter is to be found in various forms of the mark.

T. G. Green & Co. Ltd
Church Gresley, Nr. Burton-on-Trent, c.1864 onwards.
The printed 'church mark', first registered in 1888 and used in various forms afterwards. 'England' added after 1891.

Hicks, Meigh & Johnson
Shelton, 1822–1835.
Printed mark c.1822–1835, but possibly used also by Hicks & Meigh (1806–1822). The three initial letters appear in various other printed marks.

Specialising in transfer printing under and over the glaze, and particularly in deep, dark blue underglaze.

Hilditch & Son
Lane End, 1822–1830.
Various forms of printed marks bearing initials.

Samuel Hollins
Shelton, c.1784–1813.
Impressed marks, but many pieces are unmarked.

S.HOLLINS

HOLLINS

Noteworthy for his red and chocolate-coloured unglazed stoneware decorated with raised designs in the Elers style, and for green stoneware tea- and coffee-pots decorated with applied blue jasper ornament. Many of these designs were copied from silver shapes. The use of lustre bands, particularly around the rims of mugs and tankards, and not unlike gun-metal in appearance, was a speciality of Hollins, one of the early proprietors of the New Hall porcelain works.

Johnson Bros (Hanley) Ltd
Hanley, from 1883, and at Tunstall, c.1899–1913.
Most marks, impressed or printed, are of this name mark type, and some incorporate pattern names.

Lowesby Pottery
Leicestershire, c.1835–1840.
1. & 2. Impressed, c.1835–1840.
3.   Printed, c.1835–1840.

LOWESBY		
1	2	3

Under Sir Francis Fowke, red terracotta ware covered with dull black was manufactured, and brightly painted with enamels, this painting possibly not being done in the actual factory.

Leeds Pottery
Hunslet, Leeds, under various proprietors, c.1758–1880.
1.   Impressed, c.1775–c.1800. The same words in lower case letters on printed creamware c.1790 onwards.
2. & 3. Impressed, c.1781–1820.

LEEDS POTTERY	HARTLEY, GREENS & CO.	HARTLEY GREENS & CO LEEDS•POTTERY
1	2	3

Although ordinary earthenwares and black basalts were made by the various proprietors, the fame of Leeds rests upon its fine creamware, much of which is unmarked. At first imitative of Wedgwood ware and intending to rival porcelain in lightness, durability and cheapness, the best Leeds creamware often surpasses Wedgwood in its design and technical excellence. Much is finely pierced and is so greatly admired by collectors that it is often forged. But modern copies lack the fine potting, are heavier in weight, and have a thick, white, glassy glaze unlike that of true Leeds, which has a greenish tint in the crevices.

Martin Brothers

Fulham and Southall, London, 1873–1914. The brothers were Robert Wallace, Walter, Edwin and Charles.

1. Incised, 1873–1874. 'C3' refers to the model.
2. Incised, 1874–1878. Note that the letter before the numeral is discontinued.
3. Incised, c.1878–1879.
4. Incised, c.1879–1882.

All four brothers had formal artistic training, and Walter and Edwin had been employed at Doultons. Although their productions of salt-glazed stoneware included everyday vases, bottles, bowls, jugs, etc. in the Doulton style, their fame rests most upon their grotesque, sometimes almost ugly, caricatures of human faces, birds and beasts in the shape of jugs and other suitable forms.

Charles James Mason & Co.

Patent Ironstone China Manufactory, Lane Delph, 1829–1845.
Previously G. M. and C. J. Mason, and subsequently C. J. Mason.

1. & 2. Versions of the standard ironstone mark used by G. M. and C. J. Mason 1813–1829, and subsequently throughout the life of the factory, being used after 1862 by Ashworths who later added their own name. The word 'improved' occurs c.1840.
3. A version of the basic mark, but without the scroll, c.1845.
4. Printed mark, c.1825, with pattern numbers beneath. There are several other printed marks of the period 1829–1845 using the same words.

1   2   3   4

'Mason's Patent Ironstone China' was introduced in an attempt to provide the industrial middle-class with a cheap, durable, colourful substitute for the splendid Chinese porcelain owned by the wealthy. Articles included enormous vases, some of them replicas of the Oriental, fireplace surrounds, bedposts, large dinner services and, of course, many sizes of the typical octagonal jug with snake or dragon handle. Much of the decoration was transferred and washed in with enamels, and the sometimes garish blues, reds and greens enriched with gilding of good quality. Occasionally one finds better pieces bearing panels of well-painted landscapes or flowers. A class of ware which is seldom marked is completely covered with a deep blue enamel (which usually trespasses a little upon the white base of the article), upon which decoration is applied in gold, sometimes tooled, in bright enamels, or in a combination of both.

Elijah Mayer

Cobden Works, Hanley, c.1790–1804. Succeeded by Elijah Mayer
& Son, 1805–1834.
1. Impressed, c.1790–1804.
2. Impressed or printed, 1805–1834.

E. MAYER   '**E. Mayer & Son**'

1   2

Middlesborough Pottery Co.

Middlesborough-on-Tees, 1834–1844.
An example of the anchor mark, found either with initials or with
the name in full, which in turn may be found without the anchor

Minton

Stoke, under various names, 1793 onwards.
1. Moulded, on moulded wares c.1830–1840.
2. Printed, c.1900–1908.

1   2

Thomas Minton (1765–1836) was formerly an engraver at Spodes, after
serving an apprenticeship at Caughley under Thomas Turner, for whom he
engraved several underglaze-blue designs, including the well-known
Broseley Dragon. Stone china was made at Mintons, very similar to that
introduced by Mason, decorated mainly in Oriental style, as in the case of
the famous Amherst Japan pattern made in honour of Lord Amherst,
Governor General of India.

Bernard Moore
Wolfe Street, Stoke, 1905–1915.
1. Painted mark found in various forms, 1905–1915.
2. Painted or printed, sometimes with the year, 1905–1915.
Bernard Moore's factory should not be confused with that of the
Moore Brothers (1782–1905) who preceded him, and whose wares
bear self-explanatory impressed or printed marks.

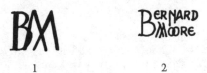

1   2

Few potters have imitated so successfully the Chinese 'sang-de-boeuf',
plain or flambé, sometimes bearing designs in blue, black, turquoise, gold
and other bright colours. Moore was able to produce a wide range of
splashed or transmutation glazes, including a fine 'peach bloom', often as
brilliant as the true Chinese.

Myatt Pottery Co.
Bilston, Staffs.
The impressed mark, registered in 1880 and used until c.1894.

MYATT

Not to be confused with the name mark used by other potters of the same
name working in the Potteries during the late eighteenth and nineteenth
centuries.

254

James Neale & Co.
Church Works, Hanley, c.1776–c.1786. Subsequently Messrs. Neale & Wilson and, in 1795, Robert Wilson.

1. Impressed mark of James Neale & Co., c.1776–1786. Impressed initials and names also used.
2. Impressed, with crescent or G, used by Neale & Co., c.1780–1790.
3. Impressed, c.1784–1795.
4. Impressed, c.1795–1800.

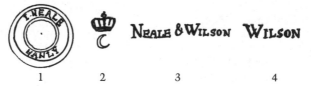

| 1 | 2 | 3 | 4 |

Makers of fine figures, usually in the classical style, since the famous French modeller Voyez worked at the factory. In addition, stoneware jugs with cupids in relief, baskets and, rather later, after Wilson joined the firm, an improved creamware, silver lustre and pink lustre in the Wedgwood style.

Pearson & Co.
Chesterfield, est. 1805.
Impressed and printed, c.1880. Before this date impressed marks 'P&CO' or the name in full.

Benjamin Plant
Lane End, Longton, c.1780–1820.
Incised mark c.1780–1820. Many other potters of the same name
worked in Staffordshire towards the end of the nineteenth century,
for the most part using name marks.

*B Plant
Lane End.*

Portobello
Near Edinburgh, c.1764 onwards.
Mark of Thomas Rathbone & Co., from 1810 onwards. Other
Portobello potters were Scott Brothers, 1786–1796, and A. W. Buchan
& Co. Ltd, from 1867 onwards, whose marks are self-explanatory.

F. & R. Pratt & Co. Ltd.
*Fenton, est. c.1818. Taken over by the Cauldron Potteries Ltd in
the 1920s. Formerly Felix Pratt.*
1.   Printed, c.1818–1860. Other marks are initials, and
        initials with '& Co' added c.1840.
2. & 3. Printed, on coloured transfer-printed wares of the 'pot lid'
        type, sometimes with pattern numbers.

PRATT   PRATT   F&R PRATT & Co
                 FENTON   268
                                FENTON

1   2   3

Above all, a company noted for the production of underglaze printed lids of pomade pots called 'pot lids', and of dessert services and other domestic wares upon which the same pot lid prints were often used. Many engravers such as the William Brooke mentioned by Simeon Shaw and Austin of Pratts, did much to develop the new process, in which every colour was printed separately, each being allowed to dry for a day or so, in contrast to the quicker and cheaper lithographic process.

Rockingham Works
Swinton, Yorkshire, c.1745–1842.

1. An impressed mark of John and William Brameld, c.1778–1842. Many other impressed marks, some including the word 'Rockingham'.
2. Impressed, c.1806 onwards.
3. Relief mark, c.1806 onwards.

BRAMELD ROCKINGHAM

  1   2   3

Best known of the earthenware made at Swinton is the brown-glazed creamware used extensively between about 1796 and 1806, and usually called Rockingham Ware, though in fact it was made also at other Staffordshire potteries. Among typical pieces are many kinds of brandy flasks in the shapes, for example, of shoes, pistols, Toby jugs, etc., and the famous peach-shaped 'Cadogan' teapot.

Royal Essex Pottery

Also known as Hedingham Art Pottery. Castle Hedingham, Essex, 1864–1901.

Applied mark in relief used 1864–1901 on so-called 'Castle Hedingham' wares, and often removed in fraudulent attempts to pass them off as much earlier pieces. An incised mark including the proprietor's name is also found.

Ralph Salt

Marsh Street, Hanley, c.1820–1846.

Impressed on scroll in relief on the backs of bases of figures.

Salt was born in 1782 and died in 1846, and was one of the most notable figure makers in the Walton style, his models being similar in design and in colouring, though he occasionally used metallic lustre either by itself or with enamels. A feature of some of his figures is the title impressed on the front of the base.

Scott Brothers

Portobello, near Edinburgh, c.1786–1896.

An example of the various impressed name marks.

SCOTT BROS

Shorthose & Heath
Hanley, c.1795–1815.
Impressed or printed, c.1795–1815.

**SHORTHOSE &
HEATH**

Shorthose & Co.
Hanley, successors to Shorthose & Heath, c.1817–1822.
Printed in blue on blue-printed wares. The name mark without
the crescents is also found, in upper case letters, in impressed,
printed and painted forms.

Shorthose & Co
CC

Notably makers of white earthenware printed overglaze in red, of rustic
subjects such as 'Children at Play' and of creamware including plates and
dishes with embossed wickerwork pierced rims.

Spodes
*Stoke-on-Trent. Various titles – Josiah Spode, c.1784–1833,
Copeland & Garrett, 1833–1847, W. T. Copeland & Sons Ltd, 1847
to present day.*
1. & 2. Impressed on blue-printed wares, c.1784–1800.
3.   Impressed on the 'New Stone' body, c.1805–1820.
4.   Printed in black, c.1805–1815, in blue, c.1815–1830.
5.–7.   Printed, c.1805–1833.
8.   Printed, 1867–1890.

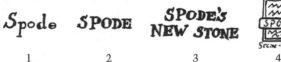

Spode	SPODE	SPODE'S NEW STONE	
1	2	3	4

5   6   7   8

Among the many achievements of this great pottery were great advances made in the process of transfer printing, not only in underglaze blue, but also in colour, particularly when applied to the durable stone chinas. Much use was made of printed outline, which was then filled in with enamels in many different colour schemes to give wide ranges of cheaply produced patterns.

Andrew Stevenson
Cobridge, c.1816–1830.
1. Impressed, c.1816–1830, and also found with initial.
2. Impressed, c.1820.
3. Impressed, c.1816–1830.

1   2   3

Ralph Stevenson
Cobridge, c.1810–1832.
One of numerous impressed marks. Sometimes the initial only, and sometimes with '& Son'.

R. STEVENSON

Stevenson & Williams
Cobridge, c.1825. According to Godden, a partnership between Ralph Stevenson and Aldborough Lloyd Williams.
1. Printed mark.
2. Printed mark on pieces decorated with American views.

Stubbs & Kent
Longport, c.1828–1830.
Impressed or printed. Also used by Joseph Stubbs of Longport, who was probably connected in some way with this firm. His wares usually bear impressed name marks, and may be dated c.1822–1835.

Swansea

Cambrian Pottery, c.1783–1870.

1.–4. Impressed, c.1783–c.1810.
5. Impressed or printed, c.1811–1817, in various forms.
6. Impressed, c.1824–1850.
7. Printed, c.1862–1870, in various forms.

SWANSEA CAMBRIA CAMBRIAN
1   2   3

CAMBRIAN POTTERY DILLWYN & CO.
4   5

DILLWYN   D. J. EVANS & CO.
6   7

It should be noted that for part of this time a rival pottery at Glamorgan (c.1814–1839) made 'opaque china' and creamware. Among Cambrian Pottery products were fine black basalt, underglaze blue-painted, blue-printed and black-printed wares, a red earthenware impressed with classical subjects in black called 'Dillwyn's Etruscan Ware' made between 1847 and 1850, and above all, an improved, whiter creamware enamelled by W. W. Young, Thomas Pardoe, and other outstanding artists.

W. Howson Taylor

Ruskin Pottery, Smethwick, Birmingham, 1898–1935.

1. Impressed, c.1898–early nineteenth century.
2. & 3. Painted or incised of the same period. Later marks are self-explanatory.

TAYLOR

1   2   3

Howson Taylor's 'Ruskin' pottery was an attempt to rival Chinese coloured glazes in every colour from white to sang-de-boeuf, often with fine flambé effects.

Charles Tittensor
Shelton, c.1815–1823. Various partnerships.
Printed on printed wares, and impressed on very rare figures.

TITTENSOR

Maker of figures with bocage or tree backgrounds, which may be looked upon as transitional between the Wood coloured glaze ones and the enamelled variety of Walton and Salt. The few authentic specimens known are rather crudely modelled and enamelled in attractive blue, green, yellow and orange-yellow.

John Turner
Lane End, Longton, c.1762–1806. Not to be confused with Thomas Turner of Caughley.
1. Impressed mark from c.1770 onwards, usually on stonewares.
2. Printed or impressed from 1784, sometimes with the name beneath.

1

2

One of Wedgwood's rivals in the making of fine jasper wares in the classical style, and a maker of fine stoneware of warm biscuit tint, sharply modelled in relief, and often enhanced with bands of blue or brown enamel. His black basalts are equal to those of Wedgwood and he is said to have been a pioneer of underglaze-blue printing in the Potteries.

John Voyez
Staffordshire modeller to Ralph and other members of the Wood family, c.1768–1800.
An example of the various impressed name marks, on such modelled specimens as the 'Fair Hebe' jug.

J.VOYEZ

A typical example of the nomadic craftsman who worked for many potters, including Wedgwood and Neale & Co.

John Walton
Burslem, c.1818–1835.
Impressed mark on a relief scroll on the backs of bocage figures.

Probably the most important potter to follow the figure-making tradition of the Woods, making gay, colourful and attractive figures with bocage backgrounds in emulation of Chelsea and Derby porcelain. His pieces were intended to be the poor man's porcelain, and were designed to stand against the wall and so to be viewed only from the front. His range of subjects was wide – religious, historical, sporting, and rustic, and he often assembled a series of stock motifs, such as cows, dogs, sheep or human figures, into different composite models.

John Warburton
Cobridge, c.1802–1825.
Impressed. The name is also found but usually with the addition
of initials and/or place names, on wares made by others of the
same name, e.g. John Warburton of Gateshead, c.1750–1795,
Peter Warburton of Cobridge, c.1802–1812, and Peter and Francis
Warburton of Cobridge, c.1795–1802.

WARBURTON

Watson's Pottery
Prestonpans, Scotland, c.1750–1840.
Impressed, c.1770–1800. Self-explanatory marks thereafter.

WATSON

Josiah Wedgwood & Sons Ltd.
Burslem, c.1759, Etruria, c.1769, Barlaston, 1940.
1.–3. Impressed marks. 1. and 3. c.1759–1769, and 2. the standard
mark c.1759 onwards. From 1860, a three-letter dating
system was used and from 1891 'England' was added. 'Made
in England' signifies a twentieth-century origin.

Wedgwood   WEDGWOOD   WEDGWOOD
1   2   3

4. Impressed on ornamental wares of the Wedgwood and Bentley period, c.1768–1780.

WEDGWOOD & BENTLEY

4

5. Impressed on small cameos, plaques, etc., Wedgwood and Bentley period, c.1768–1780.

W&B

5

6. Impressed or in relief on vases etc. of the Wedgwood and Bentley period, c.1768–1780.

6

7. Modern mark, impressed, c.1929 onwards.

WEDGWOOD

7

8. & 9. Misleading marks of Wedgwood & Co. Ltd, Unicorn and Pinnox Works, Tunstall, c.1860 onwards, and John Wedge Wood of Burslem and Tunstall, c.1845–1860.

WEDGWOOD & CO.   J.WEDGWOOD

8   9

Apart from his fame as a developer of the classical spirit in his wonderful jasper ware, Wedgwood also brought creamware to a high standard of excellence for domestic use. He also invented or improved variegated wares which imitated marble and other natural stones, the red ware called 'rosso antico', which was sometimes decorated with bright enamels, and the well-known, clean-looking 'cauliflower' wares.

Enoch Wood

Burslem, c.1784–1790.

1.–3. Examples of the various name marks on domestic wares, figures, plaques, etc. Though a modeller of note, he did not set up a factory of his own until 1784.

ENOCH WOOD SCULPSET	E WOOD	Enoch Wood &Co
1	2	3

Known in his day as the 'Father of the Potteries', and a capable potter and modeller besides being one of the first recorded students and actual collectors of early pottery. He is best known for his portrait busts in black basalt, black-enamelled creamware and painted creamware, and his vast output also included blue-printed earthenwares bearing landscapes and figure subjects intended for the American market.

Wood & Caldwell

Burslem, c.1790–1818. Successors to Enoch Wood.
Impressed mark.

WOOD & CALDWELL

Enoch Wood & Sons

Burslem, 1818–1846. Successors to Wood & Caldwell.
Impressed. Other self-explanatory name marks also used.

Other Marks

Registration Marks
1842–1883

A diamond-shaped mark, printed or impressed, is often seen on wares first made between 1842 and 1883, indicating that to prevent piracy a particular design of an article had been registered with the London Patent Office. It will of course be clear that the information thus given in the marks will only indicate the earliest possible date of manufacture, since the design so registered could have been used in succeeding years.

Year letters in top angle of diamond
1842–1867

A 1845	G 1863	M 1859	S 1849	Y 1853
B 1858	H 1843	N 1864	T 1867	Z 1860
C 1844	I 1846	O 1862	U 1848	
D 1852	J 1854	P 1851	V 1850	
E 1855	K 1857	Q 1866	W 1865	
F 1847	L 1856	R 1861	X 1842	

Year letters in right-hand angle of diamond
1868–1883

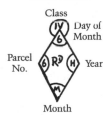

A	1871	H	1869	P	1877	X	1868
C	1870	I	1872	S	1875	Y	1879
D	1878	J	1880	U	1874		
E	1881	K	1883	V	1876		
F	1873	L	1882	W	1878		

Month letters – the same for both arrangements

A – December	H – April
B – October	I – July
C or O – January	K – November and December 1860
D – September	M – June
E – May	R – August and 1–19 Sept 1857
G – February	W – March

Registration numbers
from 1884

Numbers prefixed 'Rd.' or 'Rd. No.' are found on many wares
made from January 1884 onwards, of which a full list may be
found in G. A. Godden's *Encyclopaedia of Pottery and Porcelain
Marks*.

Minton Year Cyphers

Much Minton ware may be identified and dated by the presence of impressed year cyphers, which were introduced in 1842.

1842	1843	1844	1845	1846
✳	△	☐	✕	⬯
1847	1848	1849	1850	1851
⌒	⬌	⬳	♧	∴
1852	1853	1854	1855	1856
V	⬤	℅	✻	φ
1857	1858	1859	1860	1861
◇	⋔	⚹	⚭	人
1862	1863	1864	1865	1866
⧖	⧗	⋝	⚞	✕
1867	1868	1869	1870	1871
⋀	⊟	⊡	⒢	ℵ
1872	1873	1874	1875	1876
⊛	⋇	↓	Ɛ	⬭
1877	1878	1879	1880	1881
⬯	⬮	⬯	⬮	⊞
1882	1883	1884	1885	1886
⊗	⊙	⊠	⋈	B
1887	1888	1889	1890	1891
⚜	∞	S	T	⚘

1892	1893	1894	1895	1896
1897	1898	1899	1900	1901
1902	1903	1904	1905	1906
1907	1908	1909	1910	1911
1912	1913	1914	1915	1916
1917	1918	1919	1920	1921
1922	1923	1924	1925	1926
1927	1928	1929	1930	1931
1932	1933	1934	1935	1936
1937	1938	1939	1940	1941
1942				

The Royal Arms Mark

Many printed marks on nineteenth- and twentieth-century wares incorporate a version of the Royal Arms, often with self-explanatory names and place names. In their absence, it is difficult to attribute origin, though the actual form of the Arms themselves provides a clue as to date of manufacture. Thus, before 1837 we find an extra tiny shield in the centre, which is missing in later versions.

The Staffordshire Knot Mark

Many firms in the Potteries used the 'Staffordshire Knot' as a mark usually with distinguishing initials in the three loops. H. Aynsley & Co., H.A. & Co., 1873–1932, is a good example of this (see page 239).

Pilkington's Tile & Pottery Co. Ltd
Clifton Junction, near Manchester
c.1897–1938 and 1948–1957

Many potters have tried to emulate the lovely coloured glazes of the Orientals, among them William de Morgan, Bernard Moore, W. Howson Taylor (Ruskin Pottery) and William and Joseph Burton of Pilkingtons and the Royal Lancastrian Pottery. At the beginning of the twentieth century, the firm was probably the largest manufactory of artistic decorative tiles in the country, specialising in beautiful lustre effects. Since many items were designed by craftsmen of note, we give the marks usually found on examples of their work.

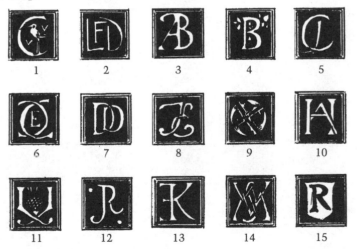

1   2   3   4   5

6   7   8   9   10

11   12   13   14   15

Wedgwood Year Letters
1860–1906

From 1860 onwards, earthenwares bear impressed three-letter year marks, the last letter denoting the year of manufacture. Thus, O–1860 to Z–1871, A–1872 to Z–1897, A–1898 to I–1906. This repetition may obviously cause some confusion, somewhat eased by the appearance of the word 'England' from 1891 onwards. These year marks are accompanied by the standard impressed 'Wedgwood' factory mark.

OLD SHEFFIELD PLATE
AND
ELECTROPLATE

Old Sheffield plate was invented in the middle of the eighteenth century when it was discovered that a thin layer of silver could be fused on to copper, producing products that looked as if they were made of solid silver but cost a fraction of the price. The designs used by the Sheffield plate manufacturers were copied from popular styles of silverware, and indeed much Sheffield Plate was made by silversmiths. The success of Sheffield plate ended in the middle of the nineteenth century with the discovery of British plate and electroplating.

The marks struck on Old Sheffield plate are not as helpful as those on silver in helping to establish the date of manufacture, and, indeed, from 1773 to 1784 they were actually forbidden in order to prevent plate being passed off as silver. Nevertheless, there are some guidelines which a collector can follow.

- A crown indicates that the item was made between 1765 and 1825.
- The words 'Best Sheffield Heavy Silver Plating' were only used after 1820.
- Genuine Old Sheffield plate that has no marks dates from between 1773 and 1784.

Distinguishing Old Sheffield Plate from Electroplate

Electroplaters often tried to make their products look like the more expensive Old Sheffield plate, but the two can be distinguished by careful inspection.

- Old Sheffield plate has a faint glow which is almost blue. If you come across a more reddish glow, the item is a more

thinly silvered foreign import. Electroplated products have a duller appearance.
- With any hollow item, the process involved in plating has to leave a seam whereas electroplating does not.
- The words 'Sheffield Plated' stamped on an item in fact mean that it is electroplated!
- The letters BP denote that the item is British plate.
- The letters EP or EPNS mean that the item is electroplated.

Electroplate

By 1842 Elkington & Co. of Birmingham had perfected the process of silver deposition on to a preformed article. The process became known as electroplating or silver plating.

The article to be plated was placed in a solution of potassium cyanide with a negative pole attached to it. The positive pole was attached to a 100 per cent pure silver sheet. A low voltage current was then passed through the solution. This allowed the silver sheet, acting as a cathode, to produce silver ions which passed into the solution and were drawn to the article, acting as an anode, adhering to its surface. The longer the process was operated, the thicker the coating of silver.

The vat containing the solution was lined with Portland cement and had to be kept extremely clean at all times for the process to work. The quality of the finish on the resulting end product depended on this, since imperfections could result from the presence of foreign bodies in the solution.

On removal from the vat, the article was gently hammered over its surface to make sure that the silver coating had adhered properly. Finally the article was burnished. The most common base metals were Britannia metal and nickel silver. Other base metals used were copper, nickel, brass and British plate.

Old Sheffield plate production quickly declined with the advent of electroplating and by the 1860s had almost ceased to be manufactured. Some Old Sheffield platers seeking to survive converted over to electroplating and went on to prosper. They produced the majority of electroplated wares and, almost without exception, stamped their marks on them. The general rule is that if it is English made and marked, it is probably Sheffield made, and if it is unmarked it is probably Birmingham made. However, beware of teasets – usually only one article, the teapot, may be marked.

A lot of modern silver plate purporting to be antique is often sold at high prices in antique shops. Conversely, truly antique pieces often trade at lower prices with the seller and purchaser none the wiser as to the authenticity of the piece.

Early pieces of electroplate, often called silver plate, are beautifully crafted and hand-engraved and are important historically. If you know what you are looking for, many bargains may be had and good investments made.

Base Metals

Copper

This was a popular base metal at the start of electroplating. However, as time wore on it was dropped due to its expense. Generally, silver-plated copper wares date from the early to mid-Victorian period and will often have the letters EP stamped on their bases to denote electroplate. Note, however, it was still used to a lesser degree in Britain by some firms right up to the twentieth century.

The metal shows through worn areas as a pinkish or sometimes reddish-brown hue.

Nickel

Pure nickel was first mined in Saxony, Germany, around 1830. The pure metal was used sparingly throughout the Victorian period but its alloy, nickel silver, was used more extensively since it is a good base metal.

The metal shows through worn areas as a light dull grey colour and wares usually have the letters EP stamed on their bases.

Nickel Silver

Also called German and in the early days Argentine silver, it actually contains no silver at all. It is an alloy of copper, zinc and nickel. German silver gets its name from the fact that nickel was first mined at Saxony in Germany.

It was soon discovered by Elkington that this alloy provided a perfect base for electroplating. It was used for this purpose from about 1842 and is still used today.

The yellow/white colour of the base metal allows easy identification on worn areas.

The words 'Hard Soldered' are occasionally seen stamped incuse on the base of the articles. Hard solder was used on electroplated wares prior to plating and is an alloy containing 50/50 nickel and silver.

Wares will have the letters EPNS or EPGS denoting electroplated nickel silver and electroplated German silver respectively. Various combinations of letters are also used, i.e. EP, NS and GS.

Understandably, the name German silver was dropped around the time of the First World War for patriotic reasons.

Britannia Metal

This alloy was developed around 1770 as a cheap alternative to Old Sheffield plate and gained increasing popularity from its inception. Around 1846 it was discovered that Britannia metal could be silver plated.

Electroplating was very appealing to the Britannia metal-smiths as the alloy plated very well and since their original plan was to produce a less expensive substitute to Old Sheffield plate, electroplating was a real bonus, for it brought them ever closer to their objective. Nearly all the 50 or so Britannia metal-makers of Sheffield had by 1880 converted to electroplating merely by the inclusion of plating vats.

By 1870, labour costs became an increased burden to the costs of manufactured goods and what with intense competition, it's not surprising that many Britannia metal firms started producing wares of poor quality, thin gauge and only a light coating of silver. It is these cheap electroplated wares produced during the late Victorian period that gave Britannia metal a bad reputation for being a base metal of cheap wares.

The letters EPBM are usually stamped on the base of wares denoting electroplated Britannia metal.

Although this alloy was used from 1846, the abbreviation EPBM didn't come into general use until 1855. In the past, goods that were badly worn were discarded as junk. However, Britannia metal, being pewter, is collectable in its own right, particularly Victorian wares that are becoming ever more sought after.

British Plate

This is a form of nickel silver. The letters BP are marked on goods denoting British plate.

Design Registration Marks

Some metal wares may be dated if their design was registered. From 1843 to 1883 diamond-shaped impressed marks contained a year letter in the top or right-hand angle.

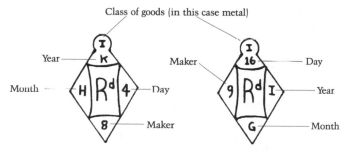

Year letter codes 1842–1867

A	1845	N	1864
B	1858	O	1862
C	1844	P	1851
D	1852	Q	1866
E	1855	R	1861
F	1847	S	1849
G	1863	T	1867
H	1843	U	1848
I	1846	V	1850
J	1854	W	1865
K	1857	X	1842
L	1856	Y	1853
M	1859	Z	1860

Year letter codes 1868–1883

A	1871	V	1876
C	1870	W	1878
D	1878	X	1868
E	1881	Z	1879
F	1873		
H	1869		
I	1872		
J	1880		
K	1883		
L	1882		
P	1877		
S	1875		
U	1874		

The months were the same for both series.

A December (except 1860	E May	K November and December 1860
B October	G February	M June
C January	H April	O January
D September	I July	R August and 1–19 September 1857
		W March

The day of the month was marked as the numbered date, i.e. the 8th was marked 8.

From 1884, registration numbers took over from the diamond registration mark.

Year registration numbers

1884	1 – 19753	1895	246975 – 268391
1885	19754 – 40479	1896	268392 – 291240
1886	40480 – 64519	1897	291241 – 311657
1887	64520 – 90482	1898	311658 – 331706
1888	90483 – 116647	1899	331707 – 351201
1889	116648 – 141272	1900–1909	351202 – 551999
1890	141273 – 163766	1910–1919	552000 – 673749
1891	163767 – 185712	1920–1929	673750 – 751159
1892	185713 – 205239	1930–1939	751160 – 837519
1893	205240 – 224719	1940–1949	837520 – 860853
1894	224720 – 246974		

Makers' and Other Marks

Most Sheffield platers stamped their initials on their wares, e.g. James Dixon & Sons stamped 'JD & S'. However some of the Britannia metalsmiths involved with electroplating stamped the company name in full or just their surname, e.g. Philip Ashberry.

Maker's Mark

Knowing who the maker is and their dates of manufacture establishes a lower and upper date of any article. Knowing when changes occurred to the company title can distinguish earlier pieces from later pieces, as when '& Sons', 'Co.' or new partners were added.

Trade Mark

Many companies had trademarks which could be registered from about 1878. For instance, James Dixon & Sons used a trumpet and banner, which were put on all their wares from 1879. Therefore, pieces not having this trademark are most definitely prior to 1879.

Misleading Initials

Beware that sometimes an I will replace J, for example some early James Dixon and John Harrison pieces have been seen with the stamp marks 'I D & S' and 'I H & Co.' respectively.

A1

This is stamped on many wares and is just a sales ploy used to imply quality.

Electroplated

This word was stamped incuse on many wares during the period 1842–1855 before the abbreviation EPNS and EPBM came into general use.

England

Never found on goods before 1890. Commonly found on ware around 1890–1920.

Made in England

Commonly found on wares from around 1920 to the present day.

Crown Inside Shield

A crown inside a shield denotes the Victorian period prior to 1897. The mark of course mimicked the crown used to assay silver at Sheffield. Its use stopped around 1897 after the guardians at the Sheffield Assay Office threatened legal action.

Plumes

Sometimes found on Victorian goods.

Initials

The majority of firms stamped their wares with their initials plus an S at the end and in a sequence of four punches to mimic sterling silver. The marks were invariably *intaglio*, that is punched in with the letters in relief. Some early marks, particularly with Britannia base metal, were stamped incuse with the company name in full.

Single Number

Usually indicating the capacity in half pints. However, it may also denote a variation in size of a particular style or even the workman's number.

Other Letters

A single or pair of letters may indicate the workman's initials.

Dating from the Styles Used

Knobs	Fruit and vegetable designs	1845–c.1890
	Bird and animal designs	1850–c.1875
	Bone, ivory and mother of pearl	1870–1880
Feet	Many designs were used throughout the Victorian period, some of which are rim, ball, lion paw, shell, claw and horse foot.	
Spouts	Fluted base	1845–1855
	Embossed leaf design	1855–1875
Body	Fruit and vegetable shapes, e.g. pear shapes were popular c.1850–c.1860, and heavily embossed bodies c.1865–c.1880.	
Borders	Shell and gadroon borders were popular throughout the Victorian period. Scroll borders became popular c.1850–c.1895.	

Victorian Techniques and Styles

It is worth noting that the style trends listed here were also followed by craftsmen making silver or pewter ware.

1840s — Many electroplated wares were cast in parts and soldered together rather than produced by spinning on a lathe.

1840–1865 — Antiquarianism. The Rococo revival came into being. From about 1840 to 1850, unembossed styles like the melon-shaped teapots were popular. From about 1850, complex embossing was employed.

1840–c.1880 — Organic naturalism was very much in vogue and involved the copying of natural objects.

1849 — Pierced articles, for example salvers, were produced no earlier than this date.

1855–1875 — Adams or Louis XVI revival period brought hanging festoons, urns, rams' heads, corn husks and paterae.

1855–1875 — Etruscan or Graeco-Roman antiquities came into fashion.

1865–1910 — Neo-classical style came into vogue, the Adams style flowing into it with typical cast bead borders with swags, paterae and scrolling foliage. Flat-chased and engraved decorations were used. Fern leaf and flower designs were very popular during this period.

1865–1890s — Japanese style.

1870–1885 — Indian style.

1870–1895 — Egyptian style.

Ethnic styles were very popular from the mid to late Victorian period.

1880s–c.1910   Arts and Crafts movement incorporating plain traditional designs not usually decorated. The period was also known as Art Nouveau. The hand-beaten appearance of planished articles was popular during this period. There are many books on the market that will explain these styles in a lot more detail.

What to Collect

If you want to collect by company name, undoubtedly the firm at the top of the list is James Dixon & Sons. Their reputation is unsurpassed by any of the other Sheffield platers. Their wares are still relatively plentiful and are thus fairly easy to collect at a modest price.

On the other hand, flatware or cutlery is far easier to collect, as huge quantities of it were produced from mid-Victorian times. For this reason, masses of it turns up everywhere for as little as 5p an item. Forget forks as they are generally not collectable, but spoons on the other hand have a devout following. Antique spoons, particularly of the seventeenth and eighteenth centuries, are very rare, expensive and are beyond the means of modest collectors who have turned their attention to nineteenth-century spoons thus including electroplated spoons in their collections.

Caution must be exercised as a lot of it is junk – avoid damaged or worn pieces, and any pieces where the silver coating has worn away. Some of the most collectable types of spoon are the caddie spoon, jam spoon and tea spoon. Spoons in the Art Nouveau style are particularly desirable to the collector of nineteenth-century spoons, but are extremely rare to find these days and are usually very expensive.

The Makers' Marks

The marks shown on the following pages are not generally shown to scale but are often enlarged to show clarity of detail. Also, variations may exist because over the years different punches may have been used.

Because the actual marks are often taken from pieces true to life, some of the detail may have been lost due to wear and tear. However, this can be excused by the fact that the marks shown are representative of the condition you are most likely to find them in.

The dates given are as accurate as can be and are based on company records and dates extensively researched at the local studies and archives department of Sheffield libraries.

Generally, the electroplaters stamped their wares with their initials using upper case letters and the ampersand (&) where necessary, in a series of four punch marks. Beware: there are exceptions and caution must be exercised.

Where there are not enough letters to make up the required number, then often unrelated letters are used and added at the end of the sequence. A very common letter used was S. John Harrison sometimes used the letters NW denoting Norfolk Works.

Britannia metal-makers sometimes stamped their wares with their full name or surname, address and the word 'Sheffield' prior to plating. Examples of companies that did this are Philip Ashberry & Sons and John Harrison.

Different companies with the same surname may or may not be related. Connections can sometimes only be inferred by date sequencing.

Introduction to the Tables

The marks illustrated in the tables on the following pages have been treated in two sections. The first contains all the marks containing initials. Where the mark contains a name, the mark is listed under the initial letter of the surname. Where the mark only contains initials, it is listed under the first initial, reading from left to right, unless another of the initials is clearly dominant. The second section contains pictorial marks. Makers marked 'OSP' are Old Sheffield plate makers. Other marks are for electroplated wares.

A

Ashford Ellis & Co.	OSP 1770	
J. Hatfield	OSP1808	
Atkin	From 1853	
Atkin	20th century	
J. Allgood	OSP 1812	
G. Ashforth & Co.	OSP 1784	
Ashley	OSP 1816	
Askew	OSP 1828	
E. Allport	OSP 1812	

B

Boulton & Fothergill	OSP 1764	
Briddon	1863–1910	
Briddon	1863–1910	
Briddon	1863–1910	

W. Banister	OSP 1808	
G. Beldon	OSP 1809	
Beldon, Hoyland & Co.	OSP 1785	
H. Best	OSP 1814	
Best & Wastidge	OSP 1816	
W. Bingley	OSP 1787	
Thomas Bishop	OSP 1830	
J. Bradshaw	OSP 1822	
Brittain, Wilkinson & Brownhill	OSP 1785	
Brumby	1889–1897	

C

J. Gilbert	OSP 1812	
J. Gilbert	OSP 1812	
J. Gilbert	OSP 1812	
Cooper	1867–1964	
Creswick	1863–1890	
Hawksworth	1867–1869	SIBERIAN SILVER
Roberts	1879–1892	
Sissons	1885–1891	
T. Cheston	OSP 1809	
T. Child	OSP 1812	
W. Coldswell	OSP 1806	
C. G. Cope	OSP	
J. Corn and J. Sheppard	OSP 1819	
J. Cracknall	OSP 1814	

T. & J. Creswick	OSP 1811	CRESWICKS
J. F. Causer	OSP 1824	CAUSER
Land	1920–1944	TRADE CIVIC MARK E. P. B. M.
Land	1945–1977	REGISTERED CIVIC TRADEMARK 8194 E. P. B. M. MADE IN ENGLAND

D

D. Not attributed	OSP 1760	
J. Dixon & Sons	OSP 1835	D S
J. Dixon & Sons	OSP 1835	D*S
J. Davis	OSP 1816	DAVIS
Deakin Smith & Co.	OSP 1785	DEAKIN SMITH & Cº
J. Dixon & Sons	OSP 1835	Dixon J

J. Dixon & Sons	OSP 1835	
J. Dixon & Sons	OSP 1835	
T. Dixon & Co.	OSP 1784	
I. Drabble & Co.	OSP 1805	
G. B. Dunn	OSP 1810	
Dixon	1890–c.1935	
Fenton	1897–c.1910	

E

Roberts	1916–1919	
Roberts	1857–1934	
W. Ellerby	OSP 1803	
S. Evans	OSP 1816	

F

Cobb	1905–c.1911	F C & Cᵒ ˢ F
Fenton	1859–1896	F.Bʀˢ
Fenton	1883–1888	F F / S F
Howard	1870–1974	F H S 1 6 8 0
T. Fox & Co.	OSP 1784	FOX PROCTOR / PASMORE & Cᵒ
H. Freeth	OSP 1816	FREETH
H. Freeth	OSP 1816	C K O HF
Frogatt, Coldwell & Lean	OSP1797	FROGGATT COLDWELL & LEAN

G

R. Gainsford	OSP 1808	GA
G. Harrison	OSP 1823	GH
G. Harrison	OSP 1823	GH F

G. Gibbs	OSP 1808	
Bishop	1894–1940	
Lee	1888–1967	G. L & Cº S SHEFFIELD ELECTROPLATE E . P . B . M
Wish	1878–1934	G W S E P B M 1 0 3 0 1
W. Garnett	OSP 1803	GARNETT
Goodman, Gainsforth and Fairbairn	OSP 1800	A GOODMAN & Cº
E. Goodwin	OSP 1795	E GOODWIN
J. Green & Co.	OSP 1799	I GREEN & Cº
J. Green	OSP 1807	GREEN
W. Green & Co.	OSP 1784	W GREEN & Cº
Graves	1900–1914	J. G. GRAVES E P N S S

H

D. & G. Holly	OSP 1821	
Henry Atkin	OSP 1823	
Henry Hall	OSP 1829	
Tudor & Leader	OSP 1760	$\mathcal{H}$ $\mathcal{T}$&$\mathcal{C}^{o}$
Tudor & Leader	OSP 1760	
W. Hutton	OSP 1839	H & S Π
Atkin	From 1853	
Atkin	From 1890	5305
Boardman	1861–1927	H.P

Fisher	1900–1920	H F & Co S
Hammond	1886–1935	H C & Co S 5 8 5 6
Harrison	1862–1897	
Harrison	1862–1909	H·B & H
Hawksworth	1853–1867	H.E &Cº
Hawksworth	1892–1894	H E &Cº Lᴰ
Walker	1868–1916	H H & J E B
Wilkinson	1843–1871	
Wilkinson	1872–1894	H.W Lᴰ Silbo
Wilkinson	1872–1894	H W Lᴰ E P B M 1928
W. Hall	OSP 1820	HALL
W. Hall	OSP 1820	
Joseph Hancock	OSP 1755	IOSᴴ HANCOCK SHEFFIELD.
M. Hanson	OSP 1810	HAN SON
J. Harrison	OSP 1809	HARRI SON:

T. Harwood	OSP 1816	
D. Hill & Co.	OSP 1806	
J. Hinks	OSP 1812	
J. Hipkiss	OSP 1808	
J. Hobday	OSP 1829	
H. Holland & Co.	OSP 1784	
Dan Holly, Wilkinson & Co.	OSP1784	
Dan Holly, Parker & Co.	OSP 1804	
D. & G. Holly	OSP 1821	
D. Horton	OSP 1808	
J. Horton	OSP 1809	
S. & T. Howard	OSP 1809	
W. Hutton	OSP 1807	
W. Hutton	OSP 1831	
W. Hutton	OSP 1837	

Joseph Hancock	OSP 1755	**IH**
G. Lees	OSP 1811	LEES?
Harrison	1843–1865	HARRISON NORFOLK WORKS SHEFFIELD 2746
Hibbert	1900–1909	S. HIBBERT & SON YUKON SILVER

I

I. & I. Waterhouse	OSP 1833	✱ ✱
John Littlewood	OSP 1772	I L PLATED
J. Rowbotham & Co.	OSP 1768	**IR**
John Winter & Co.	OSP 1765	IW 👑 🛡 🔖
Creswick	1858–1863	I.F.P C&C
Harrison	1866–1891	I H & Co
Hawksworth	1867–1911	H.H.H SIBERIAN SILVER

J

John Hoyland & Co.	OSP 1764	
J. Rodgers & Sons	OSP 1822	
J. Rodgers & Sons	OSP 1822	
J. Smallwood	OSP 1823	
Roberts, Jacob & Samuel	OSP 1765	
John Hoyland	OSP 1764	
Joseph Wilmore	OSP 1807	
Bradbury	1863–1867	
Bradbury	1889–1892	
Clarke	1894–1923	
Creswick	1853–1855	
Deakin	1871–1898	
Dixon	1848–1878	

Fenton	1868–1875	
Fenton	1875–1883	
Harrison	1843–1865	
Hawksworth	1873–1892	
Hawksworth	1873–1892	
Pinder	1877–1894	
Potter	1884–1890	
Potter	1884–1921	J. H. P.
Potter	1922–1940	J H P & S
Round	1863–1897	
Townroe	1887–1916	
Turton	1898–1909	
Turton	1898–1923	
Turton	1910–1923	

J. Johnson	OSP 1812	JOHN SON +
Jones	OSP 1824	JONES
T. Jordan	OSP	JOR DAN

K

S. Kirkby	OSP 1812	KIRKBY FOR USE

L

Levesley	c.1875–1935	L Brs S m
Levesley	c.1875–1935	L B S
J. Law & Son	OSP 1807	LAW&SON
R. Law	OSP 1807	R.LAW.
Thomas Law	OSP 1758	TL TH° LAW TL
Thomas Law	OSP 1758	TL LAW TL
Thomas Law	OSP 1758	THO'LAW & C°
A. C. Lea	OSP 1808	ACLEA

G. Lees	OSP 1811	LEES
John Lilly	OSP 1815	LILLY
Joseph Lilly	OSP 1816	JOSH LILLY
M. Linwood & Sons	OSP 1808	LIN WOOD
J. Linwood	OSP 1807	LINWOOD LINWOOD
J. Linwood	OSP 1807	LINWOOD LINWOOD
W. Linwood	OSP 1807	LINWOOD LINWOOD
J. Love & Co. and Love, Silverside, Darby & Co.	OSP 1785	I LOVE & C

M

Richard Morton	OSP 1765	MG S MG S
Richard Morton	OSP 1765	MG MG MG
Mappin	From 1873	CORPORATE MARK. M TRUSTWORTHY
Mappin	From 1900	M TRUSTWORTHY

Mappin	1861–1890	
Martin	1854–1897	
Willis	1872–1885	
F. Madin & Co.	OSP 1788	
Mappin Brothers	OSP 1850	
W. Markland	OSP 1818	
H. Meredith	OSP 1807	
J. Moore	OSP 1784	
J. Moore	OSP 1784	
F. Moore	OSP 1820	
R. Morton & Co.	OSP 1785	
Fisher	1900–1925	
Mappin	20th century	

N

Nathaniel Smith	OSP 1756	**N S**
C. Needham	OSP 1821	C NEEDHAM MAKER SHEFFIELD
W. Newbould & Son	OSP 1804	W. NEWBOULD & SONS
J. Nicholds	OSP 1808	J. NICHOLDS
Nodder	1863–1904	5 JOHN NODDER & SONS SHEFFIELD 2352
Nodder	1897–1904	NODDERS SILVER

O

T. Oldham	OSP 1860	T OLDHAM MAKER NOT PLATED
Nodder	1897–1904	OSMIUM SILVER

P

J. Gilbert	OSP 1812	
J. Prime	OSP 1839	
J. Prime	OSP 1839	
Ashberry	1861–1890	
Ashberry	1867–1935	
Ashberry	1880–1935	
Pinder	1923–present	
Pinder	1877–1894	
J. Parsons & Co.	OSP 1784	
Peak	OSP 1807	
Pemberton & Mitchell	OSP 1817	
R. Pearson	OSP 1811	
J. Prime	OSP 1839	

Mappin	From 1887	
Potter	1884–1921	POTTER SHEFFIELD A1
Potter	20th century	

R

Robert & Briggs	OSP 1860	
Roberts, Smith & Co.	OSP 1828	
Richardson	1873–1924	R.R SHEFFIELD E.P.B.M 0 2 2 2 9 $\frac{1}{2}$
Roberts	1864–1867	R & B
Roberts	1864–1867	R & B
Roberts	1892–c.1920	R & B
Roberts	1920–1923	EP R AND N S
Roberts, Cadman & Co.	OSP 1785	ROBERTS & CADMAN

J. S. Roberts	OSP 1786	
J. Rodgers & Sons	OSP 1822	
J. Rogers	OSP 1819	
W. Ryland & Son	OSP 1807	

S

J. Smith & Son	OSP 1828	
J. Prime	OSP 1839	
S. Colmore	OSP 1790	
S. & T. Howard	OSP 1809	
W. Scott	OSP 1807	
Fenton	1888–1891	
Fenton	1891–1896	
Hutton	20th century	
Nodder	c.1890–1904	

Roberts	1867–1879	S R C B
T. Sansom & Sons	OSP 1821	SAN SOM
R. Silk	OSP 1809	S I
J. Shepherd	OSP 1817	SHEP HARD
T. Small	OSP 1812	SMALL
Smith & Co.	OSP 1784	SMITH&C°
Smith, Tate, Nicholson and Hoult	OSP 1810	SMITH&C°
W. Smith	OSP 1812	SM ITH
I. Smith	OSP 1821	SMITH
J. Smith	OSP 1836	JOSEPHUS SMITH
N. Smith & Co.	OSP 1784	N SMITH & C°
Staniforth, Parkinson & Co. OSP 1784		STANIFORTH PARKIN&C°
B. Stot	OSP 1811	ftot
Sykes & Co.	OSP 1784	SYKES &C°
Potter	1884–1921	SUPERIOR PLATE

T

T. Butts	OSP 1807	TB Y S 𝔅
Bradbury	1867–1878	TB JH
Bradbury	1858–1863	TB &S
Bradbury	1892–1916	T.B &S
Creswick	1852–1853	T J C &N
Land	1901–1919	T L & S S
Turner	1883–1940	TT ENCORE
S. Thomas	OSP 1818	THO MAS
E. Thomason & Dowler	OSP 1807	THOMASON
E. Thomason & Dowler	OSP 1807	
Tonks & Co.	OSP 1824	TONKS
Samuel Tonks	OSP 1807	TONKS□
Tudor, Leader & Nicholson	OSP 1784	TUDOR &Cº
S. Turley	OSP 1816	S·TURLEY

J. Turton	OSP 1820	
J. Turton	OSP 1820	
Turner	1916–1940	**T.TURNER & Co LTD** *Pedigree Plate*
J. Tyndall	OSP 1813	

W

George Waterhouse & Co.	OSP 1842	
W. Briggs	OSP 1823	
W. Hutton	OSP 1849	
W. Hutton	1843–1900	
Harrison	1857–1918	
Shirtcliffe	1921–1931	
Sissons	1858–1885	
Walker	1852–1897	

Walker	From 1862	W & H
Watson	1897–1940	W & G ... 945
W. Jervis	OSP 1789	W JER VIS
Waterhouse & Co.	OSP 1807	WATERHOUSE&C°
Watson, Fenton & Bradbury	OSP 1795	WATSON&C°
Watson, Pass & Co. (Late J. Watson)	OSP 1811	WATSON PASS&C° H
W. Watson	OSP 1833	WWATSON MAKER SHEFFIELD
W. Hipwood	OSP 1809	WHIP WOOD
J. White and White & Allgood	OSP 1811	WHITE
Joseph Willmore	OSP 1807	PATENT WILLMORES&WILKES
W. Woodward	OSP 1814	WOOD WARD X WOOD WARD X

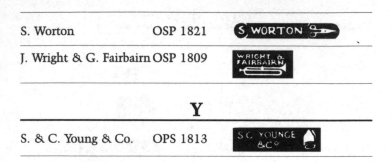

| S. Worton | OSP 1821 | |
| J. Wright & G. Fairbairn | OSP 1809 | |

Y

| S. & C. Young & Co. | OPS 1813 | |

Pictorial Marks

M. Boulton & Co.	OSP 1784	
Not attributed	OSP 1760	
Tudor & Leader	OSP 1760	
Fenton Mathews & Co.	OSP 1760	
Not attributed	OSP 1760	
John Watson & Son	OSP 1830	
Padley Parkin & Co.	OSP 1849	
Waterhouse, Hatfield & Co.	OSP 1886	
R. Sutcliffe & Co.	OSP 1786	
W. Silkirk	OSP 1807	
H. Wilkinson & Co.	OSP 1836	
Walker, Knowles & Co.	OSP 1840	
Blagden, Hodgson	OSP 1821	
Smith, Sissons & Co.	OSP 1848	

Roberts, Smith & Co.	OSP 1828	
Ashberry	1861–1915	
Atkin	From 1890	
Bradbury	1853–1897	
Creswick	1855–1890	
Creswick	1852–1855	
Deakin	1855–1891	
Dixon	1848–1878	
Dixon	1848–1878	
Dixon	1879–c.1935	

Harrison	1862–1909	HARRISON & HOWSON ALPHA SHEFFIELD 6
Hawksworth	1894 1911	HC LD
Hutton	From 1900	
Mappin	1865–1905	MAPPIN BROTHERS B
Martin	1880–1934	M H & C. EP MARTINOID 1711 3
Potter	1884–1940	SILVA
Roberts	1895–c.1920	TRADE MARK.
Rodgers	1860–1970	*+ JOSEPH RODGERS & SONS SHEFFIELD E.P.S.M X 263 2

Round	1872–1957	
Rylands	1876–c.1910	
Sissons	1858–1891	
Viners	1925–1974	
Walker	1861–1890	
Walker	1891–1909	
Walker	1910–1970	